BEGINNER VIOLA
THEORY
FOR CHILDREN
BOOK TWO

BY MELANIE SMITH

1 2 3 4 5 6 7 8 9 0

FOREWORD

In creating this workbook, I have relied on my educational experience and many years of viola as a basis for this style of instruction. With a background in both psychology and education, I have used techniques to teach children effectively while still keeping it fun — the major emphasis of learning viola at an early age. This book is designed to teach theory at a level that is attainable, yet challenging. It is intended to build confidence and solidify the relationship between theory and playing. It is written so it can be used to teach beginners the basics of theory, or even to refresh musicians who might need a small review. No matter who uses this book, it will give a strong foundation to violin and, through this understanding, will foster a greater love of playing.

TABLE OF CONTENTS

DRAWING SPACE NOTES

Draw the "G" note in space 1.

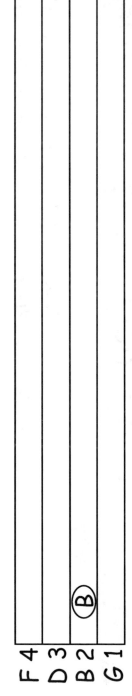

F 4
D 3
B 2
G 1 Ⓖ

Draw the "B" note in space 2.

F 4
D 3
B 2 Ⓑ
G 1

Draw the "D" note in space 3.

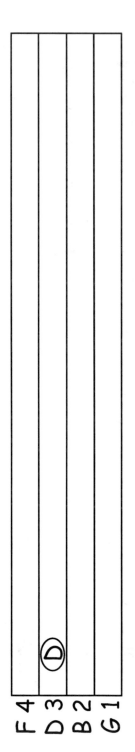

F 4
D 3 Ⓓ
B 2
G 1

Draw the "F" note in space 4.

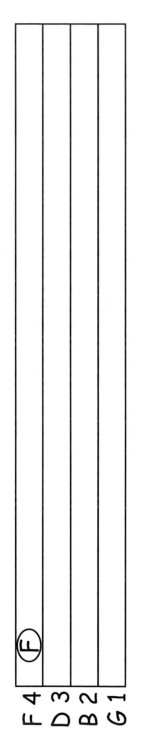

F 4 Ⓕ
D 3
B 2
G 1

Write the note name inside each note below.

* Remember: <u>G</u>randma <u>B</u>uys <u>D</u>og <u>F</u>ood

     1   2   3   4

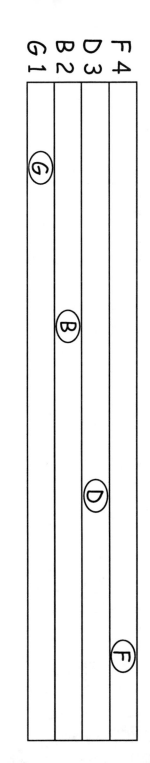

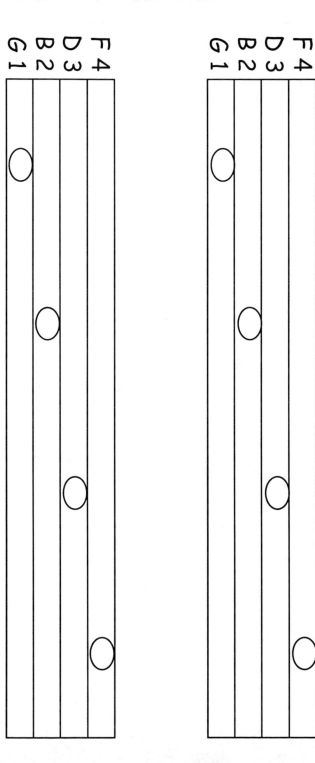

F 4
D 3
B 2
G 1

F 4
D 3
B 2
G 1

F 4
D 3
B 2
G 1

F 4
D 3
B 2
G 1

7

Write the note name inside each note below.

* Remember: <u>G</u>randma <u>B</u>uys <u>D</u>og <u>F</u>ood
        1   2   3   4

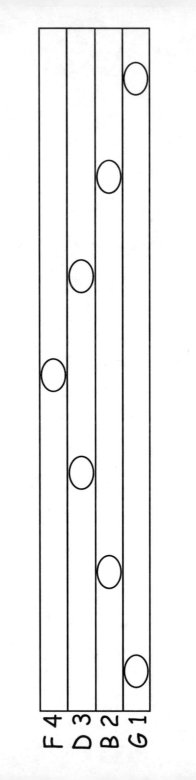

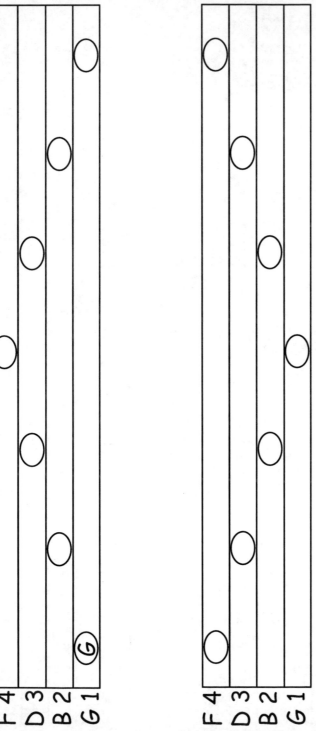

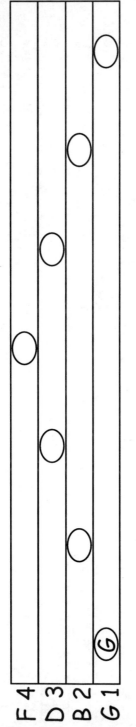

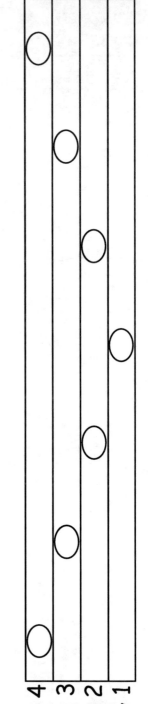

F 4
D 3
B 2
G 1

F 4
D 3
B 2
G 1

F 4
D 3
B 2
G 1

F 4
D 3
B 2
G 1

Let's mix up the notes. Write the note name inside each note below

* Remember: **G**randma **B**uys **D**og **F**ood

1   2   3   4

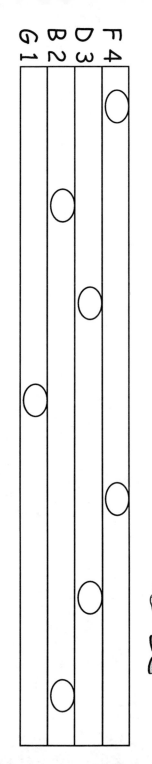

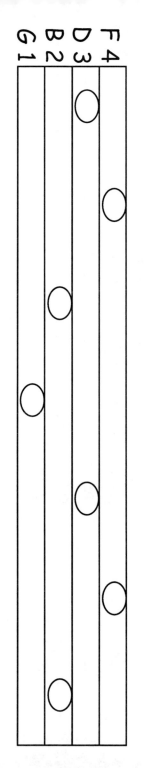

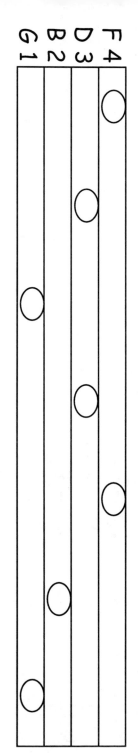

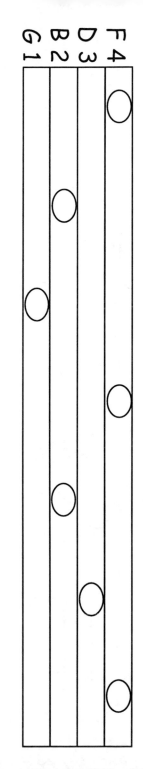

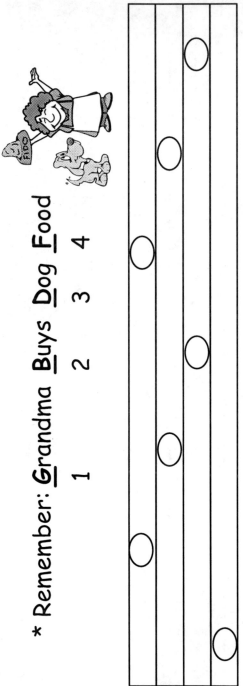

* Remember: <u>G</u>randma <u>B</u>uys <u>D</u>og <u>F</u>ood
1   2   3   4

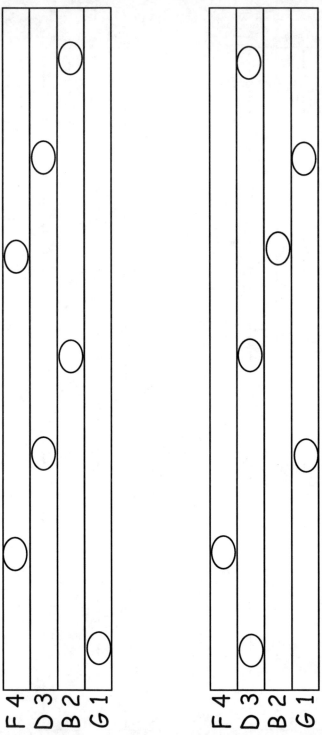

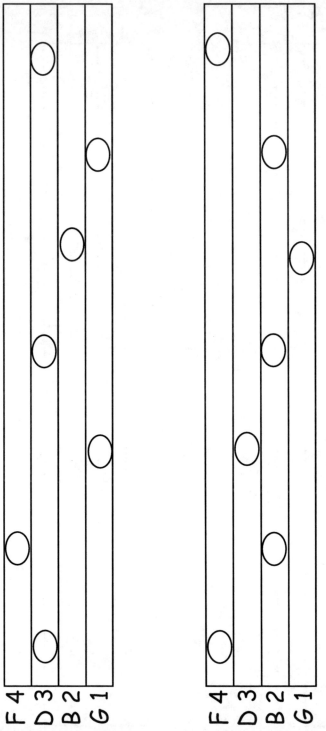

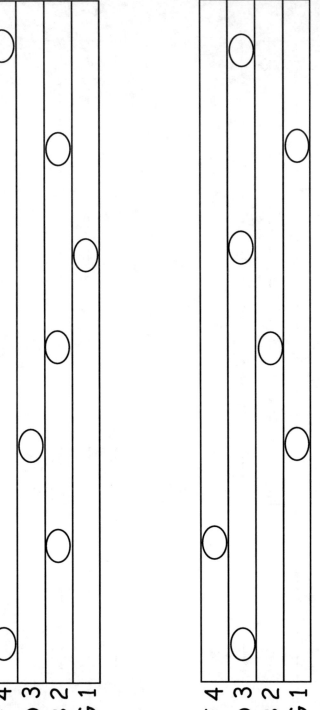

F 4
D 3
B 2
G 1

F 4
D 3
B 2
G 1

F 4
D 3
B 2
G 1

F 4
D 3
B 2
G 1

10

Use this page for extra practice.

F 4
D 3
B 2
G 1

F 4
D 3
B 2
G 1

F 4
D 3
B 2
G 1

F 4
D 3
B 2
G 1

READING MUSIC - LINE NOTES

There are _____ notes on the lines.

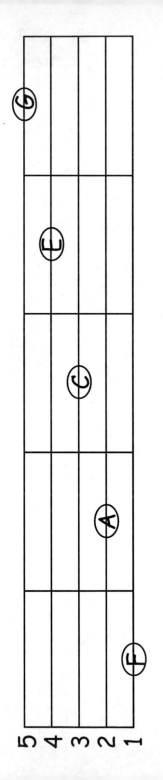

Unfortunately putting line notes together does not spell a word, but there is a saying we can use to help us remember.

The first letter in every word is the note name.

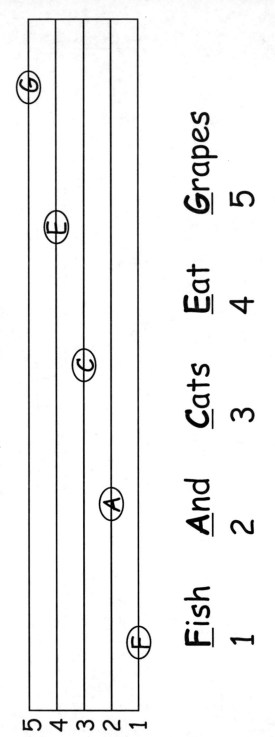

Fish	And	Cats	Eat	Grapes
1	2	3	4	5

DRAWING LINE NOTES

Draw a line across of the 'F' line note. **F is for Fish.**

Draw a line across of the 'A' line note. **A is for And.**

Draw a line across of the 'C' line note. **C is for Cats.**

Draw a line across of the 'E' line note. **E is for Eat.**

Draw a line across of the 'G' line note. **G is for Grapes.**

Use these for extra practice.

5 4 3 2 1

5 4 3 2 1

5 4 3 2 1

5 4 3 2 1

IDENTIFYING LINE NOTES

Here are the music line notes.

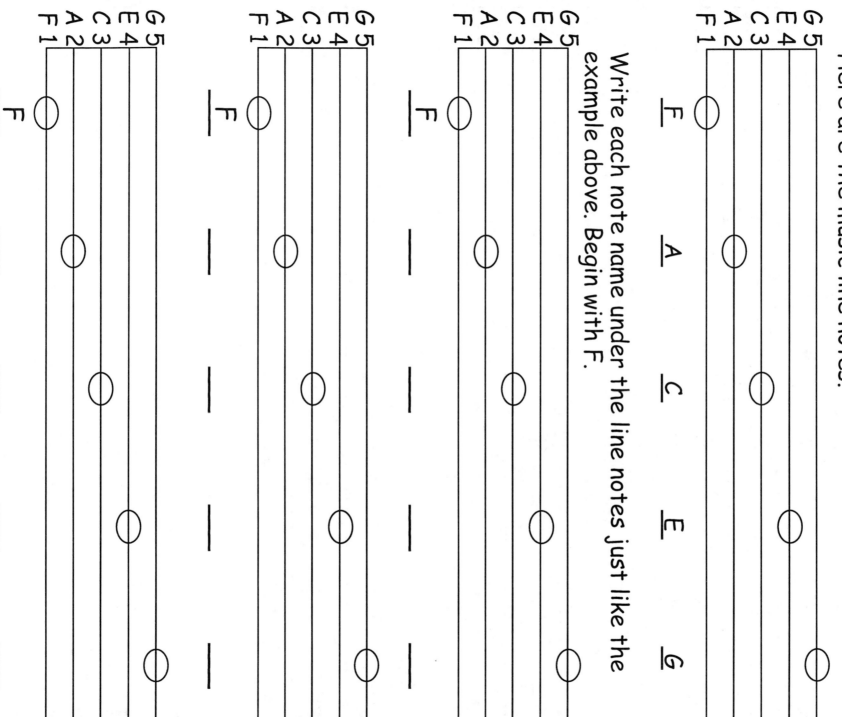

Write each note name under the line notes just like the example above. Begin with F.

Write the note name under each line note below.

* Remember: <u>F</u>ish <u>A</u>nd <u>C</u>ats <u>E</u>at <u>G</u>rapes

1   2   3   4   5

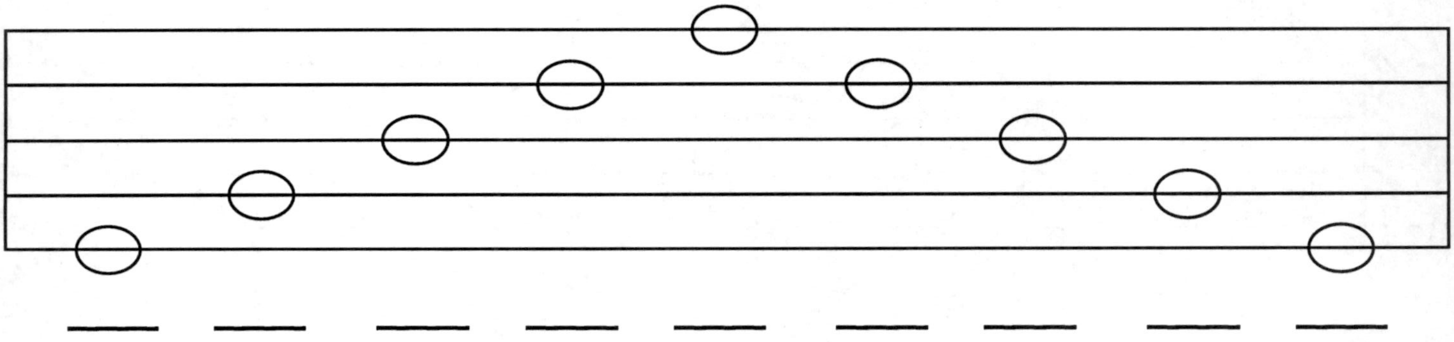

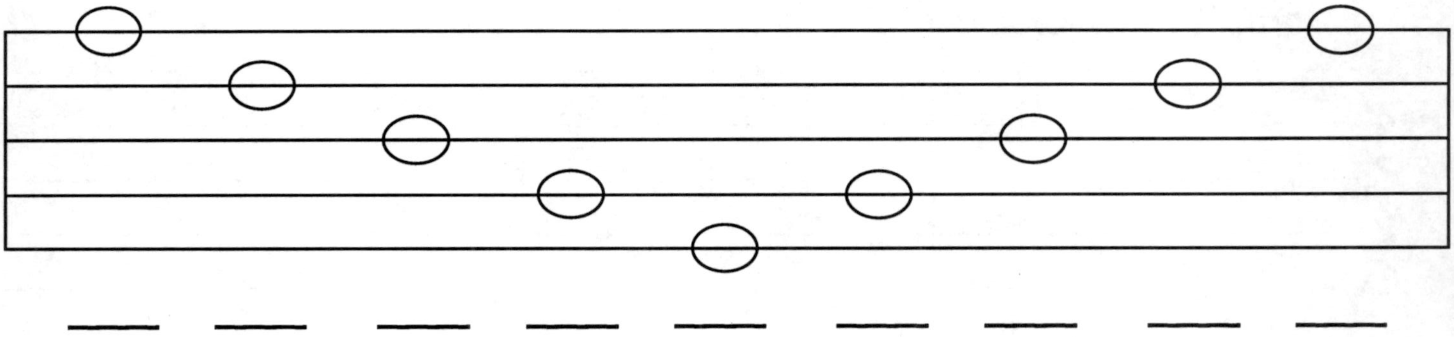

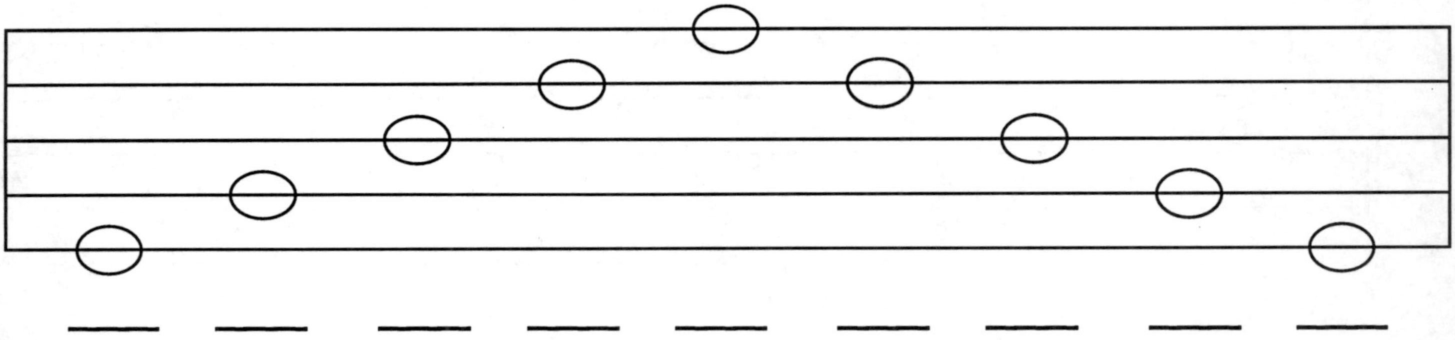

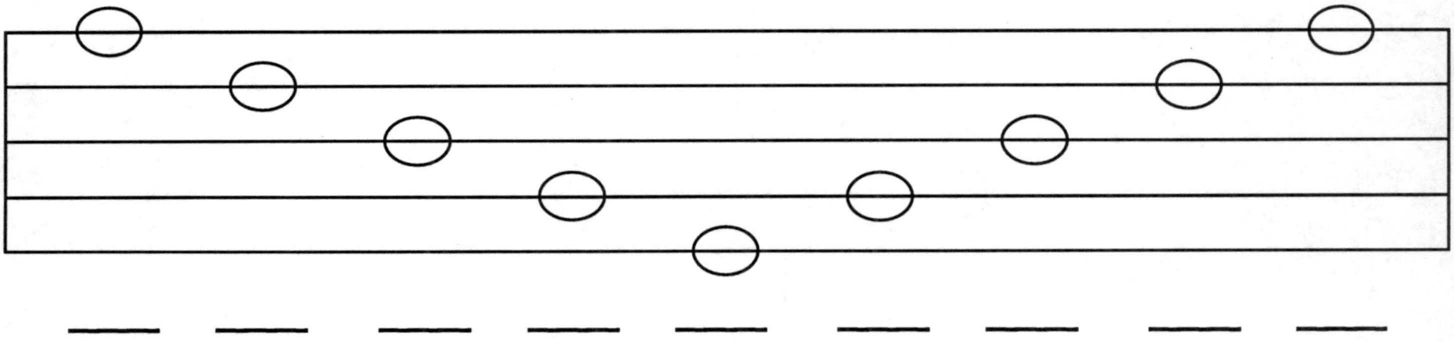

16

Write the note names below.

* Remember: <u>F</u>ish <u>A</u>nd <u>C</u>ats <u>E</u>at <u>G</u>rapes

1   2   3   4   5

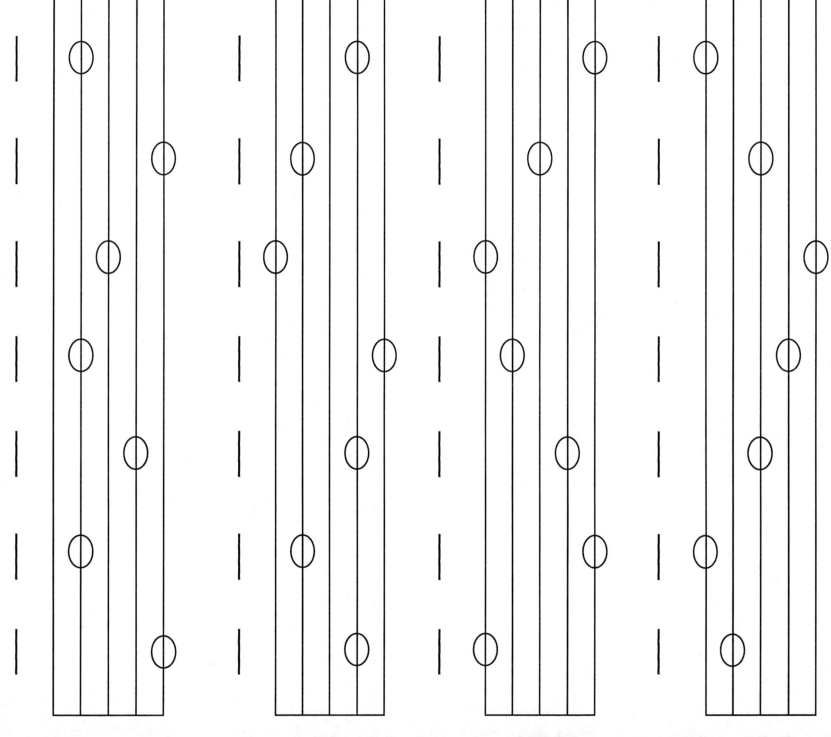

Use this page for extra practice.

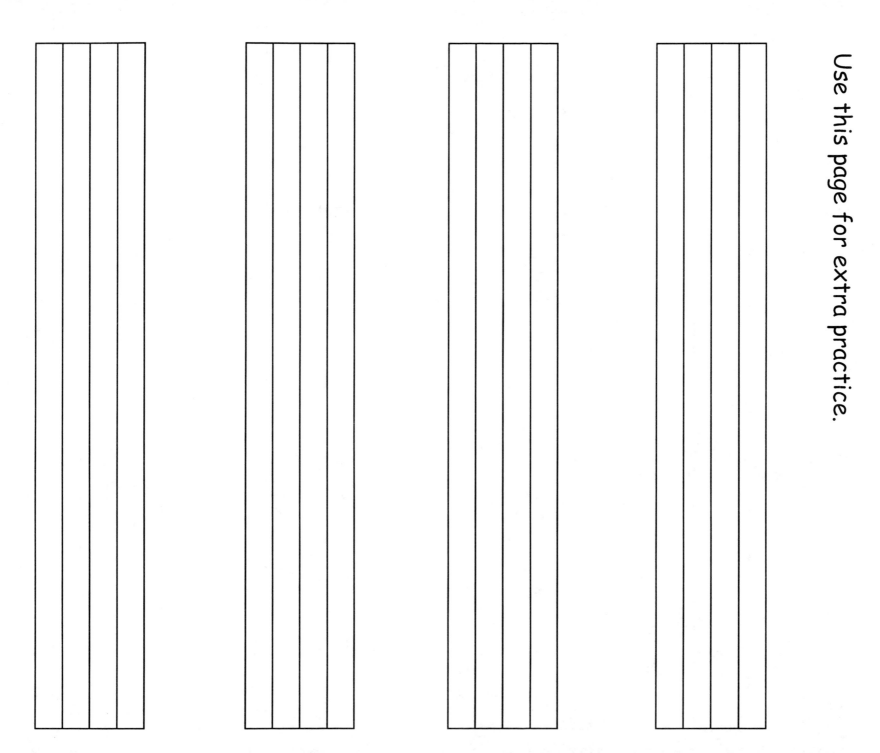

SPACE NOTE AND LINE NOTE REVIEW

What are these notes? Write their names below.

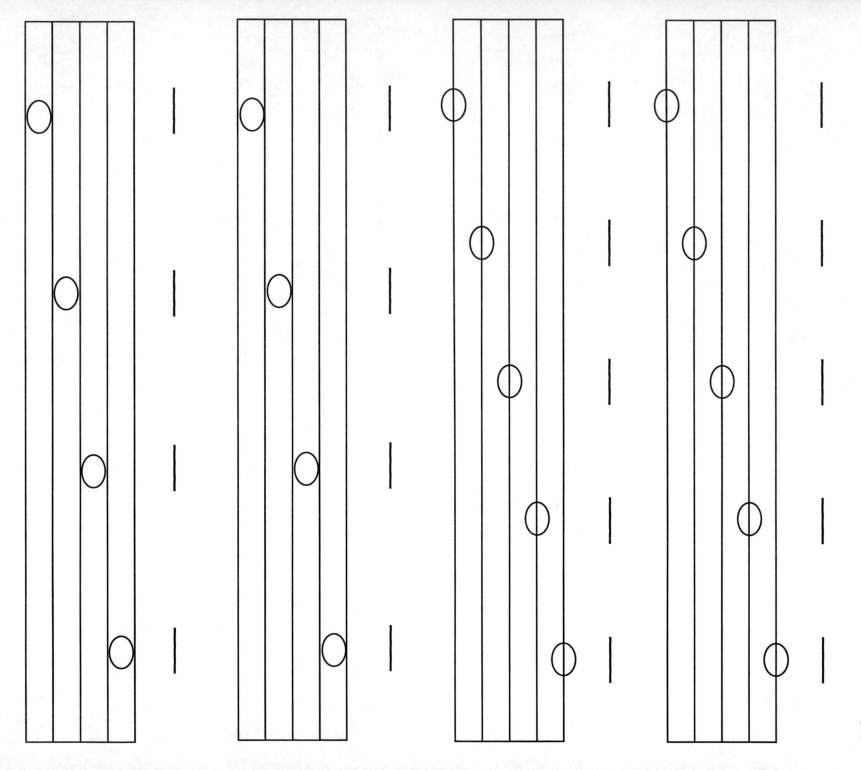

For this page, the space notes and the line notes are mixed up. Use the sayings you learned to find out what note name is and then write the note name below.

G   B   D   F
1   2   3   4

F   A   C   E   G
1   2   3   4   5

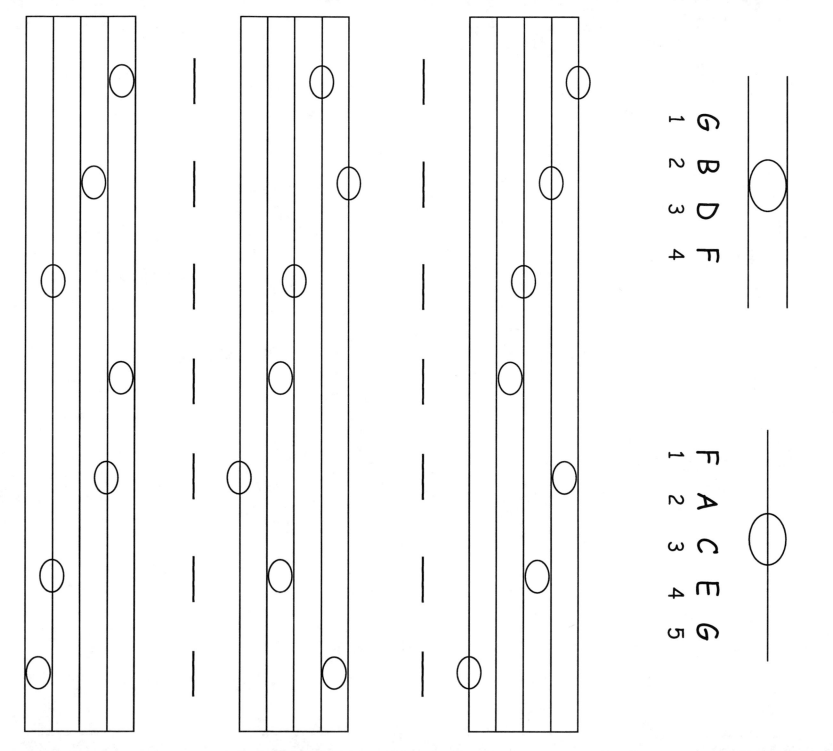

What are these notes? Write the note names below.

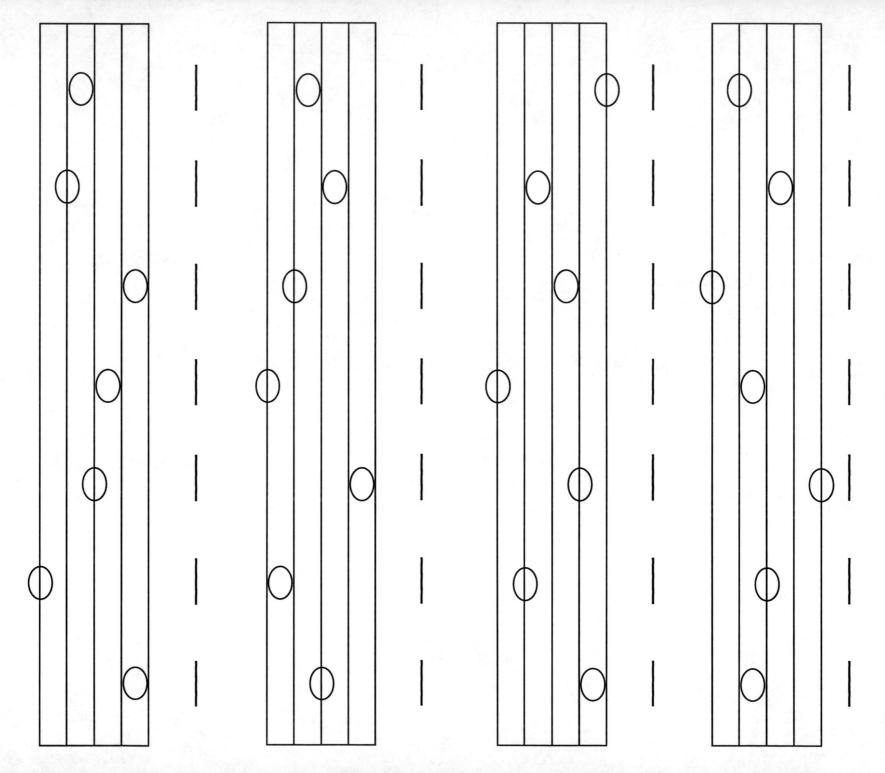

What are these notes? Write the note names below.

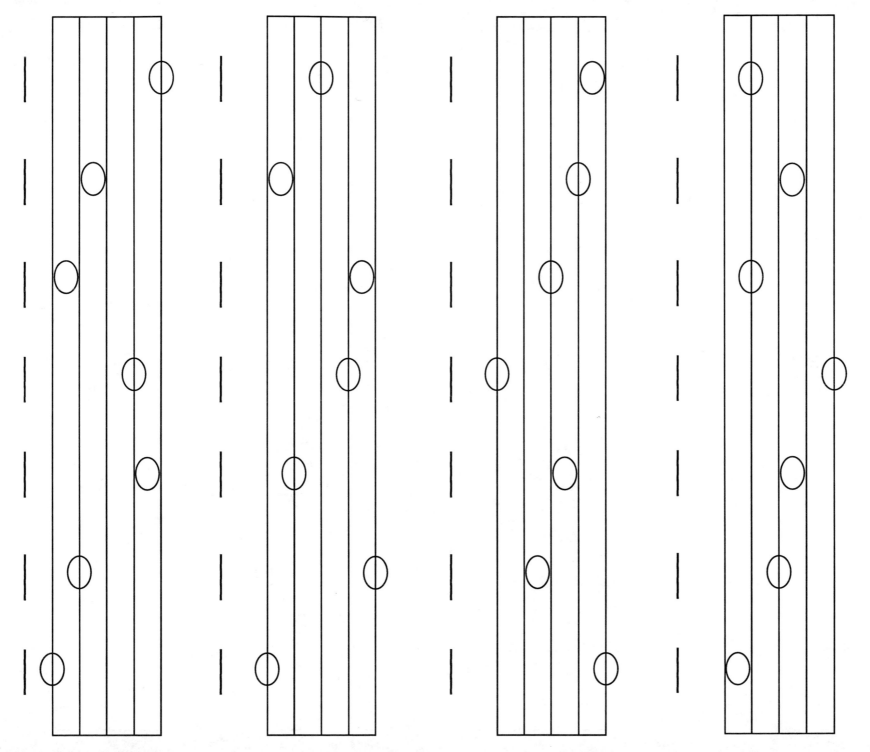

23

What are these notes? Write the note names below.

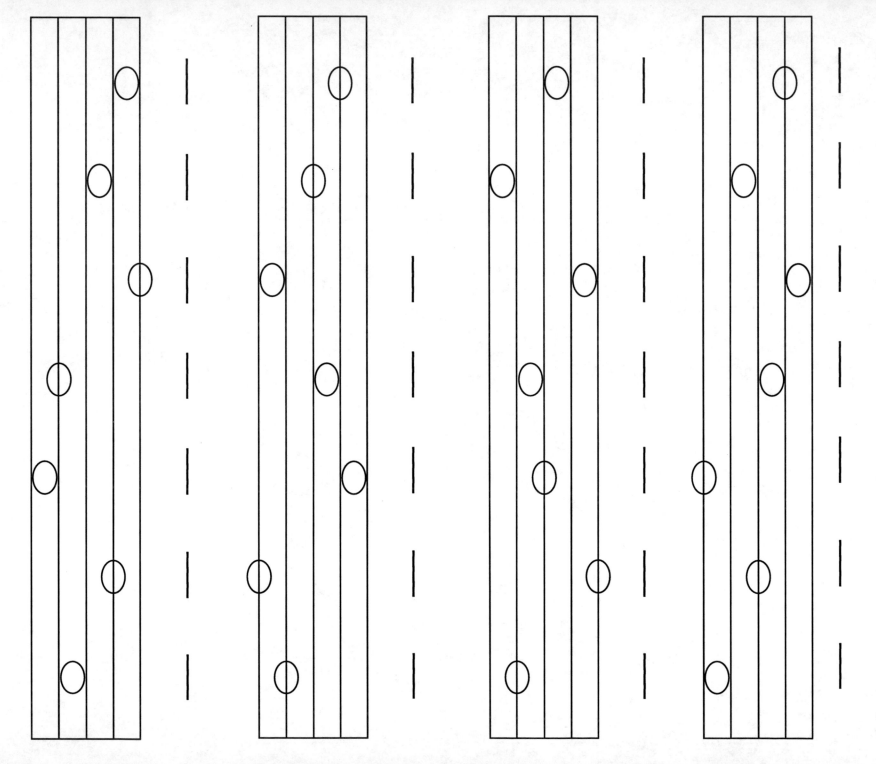

SPACE NOTE AND LINE NOTE REVIEW

Use the note names below to draw a note on the line or space where it belongs.

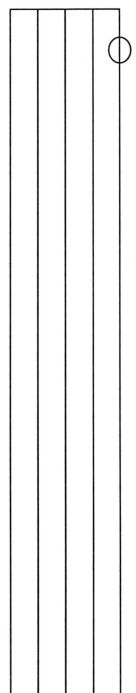

G (line)   C   G   F (line)   G (space)   B   C

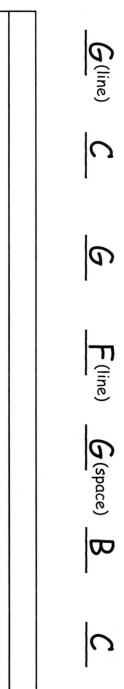

B   D   F (space)   C   A   G (space)   D

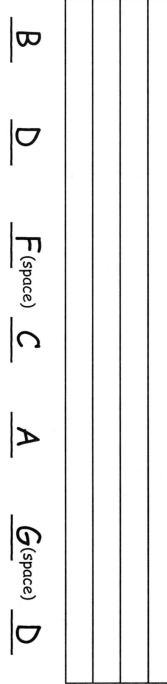

C   B   F (line)   D   G (space)   F (space)   A

B   D   A   C   G (space)   F (line)   G (line)

Use the note names below to draw a note on the line or space where it belongs.

F (space)   A   B   F (line)   G (space)   D   C

B   A   G (line)   F (space)   C   G (space)   D

C   B   C   D   F   A   G (line)

D   A   B   C   G (line)   F (line)   A

Use the note names below to draw a note on the line or space where it belongs.

D C F(space) F(line) G(space) A C

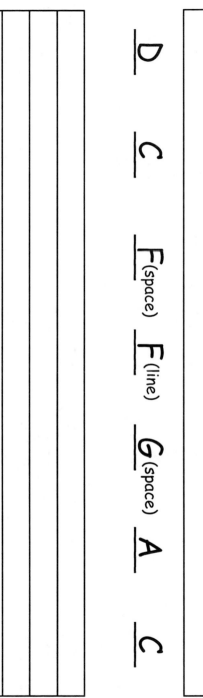

F(line) D C F(space) A G(space) D

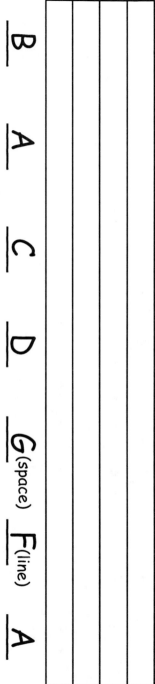

B A C D G(space) F(line) A

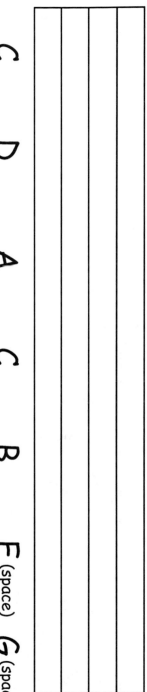

C D A C B F(space) G(space)

Use the note name to draw the note on the line or space.

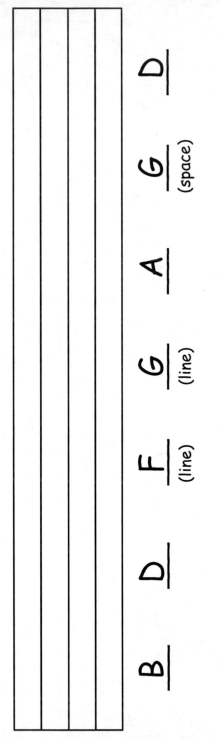

A C G F G B C
   (space) (line) (line)

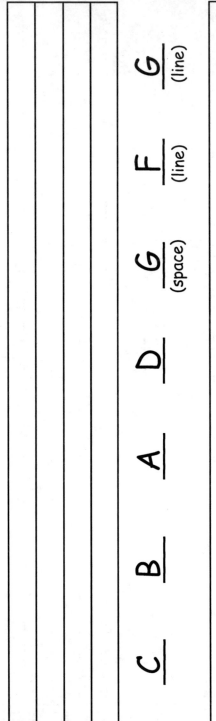

B D F G A G D
      (line) (line) (space)

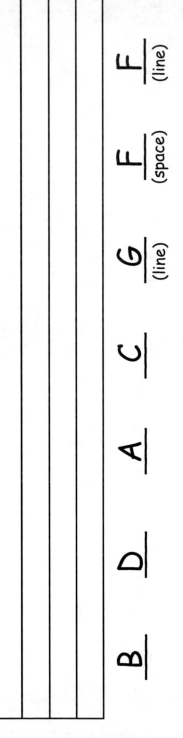

C B A D G F G
         (space) (line) (line)

B D A C G F F
      (line) (line) (space) (line)

Use the note name to draw the note on the line or space.

D | F | G | B | C | F | A
(line) | (space) | | | (space)

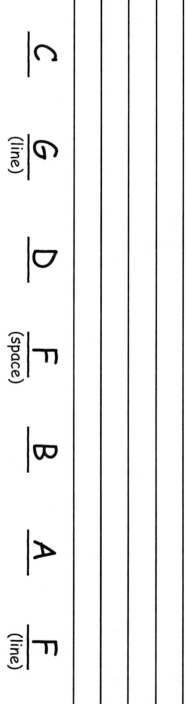

C | G | D | F | B | A | F
(line) | (line) | (space) | | (line)

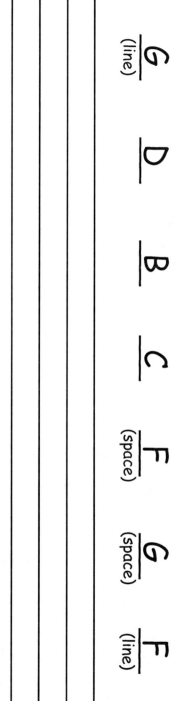

G | D | B | C | F | G | F
(line) | | | (space) | (space) | (space) | (line)

 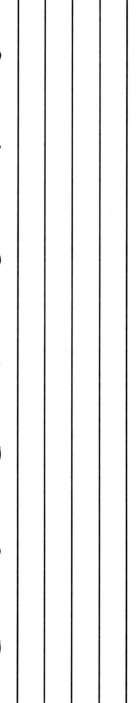

C | F | G | B | A | F | D
(line) | (space) | | | (space)

29

Use the note name to draw the note on the line or space.

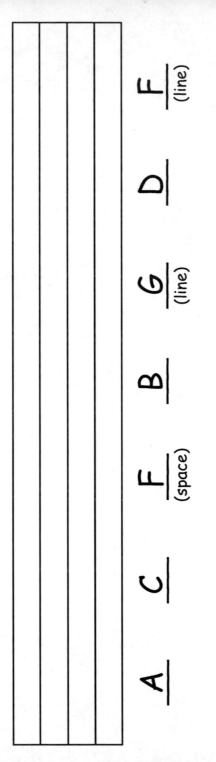

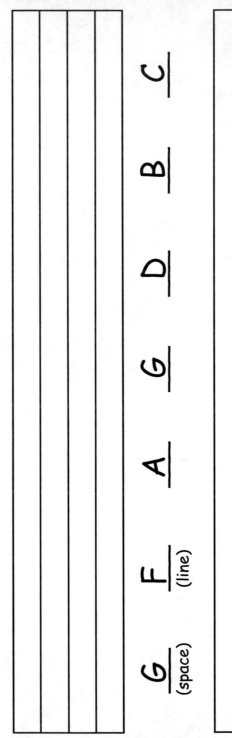

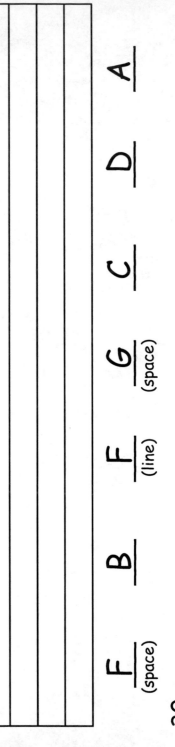

30

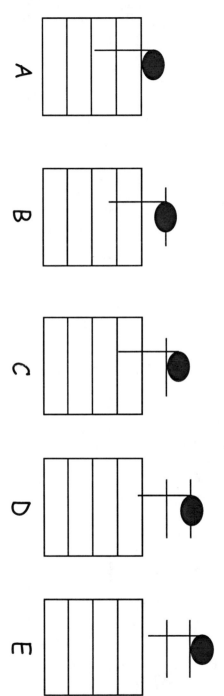

These notes are different than the ones we've seen before.

They are above the music staff.

A is on a space above the staff

B is on a leger line above the staff

C is on top of the leger line

D is on the second leger line above the staff

E is on top of the second leger line above the staff

🕷 Notice that the stem is facing down.

Draw a high 'A' note. Make sure it's on the first space above the staff.

Draw a high 'B' note. Remember to draw a leger line and draw the note on the leger line.

Draw a high 'C' note. Remember to draw a leger line and draw the note above the leger line.

Excellent Job!

Draw a high 'D' note. Remember to draw two leger lines and draw the note on the top leger line.

Draw a high 'E' note. Remember to draw 2 leger lines and draw the note above the top leger line.

Now let's practice what we've learned. Write the note names in the boxes below. Remember the notes are A, B, C, D and E.

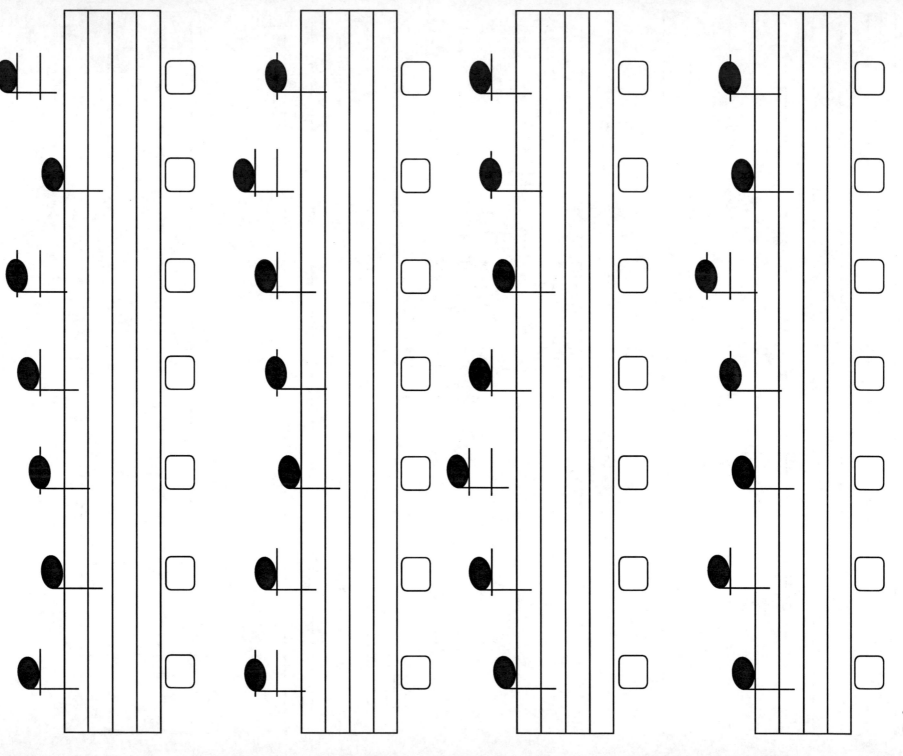

Now let's practice what we've learned. Write the note names in the boxes below. Remember the notes are A, B, C, D and E.

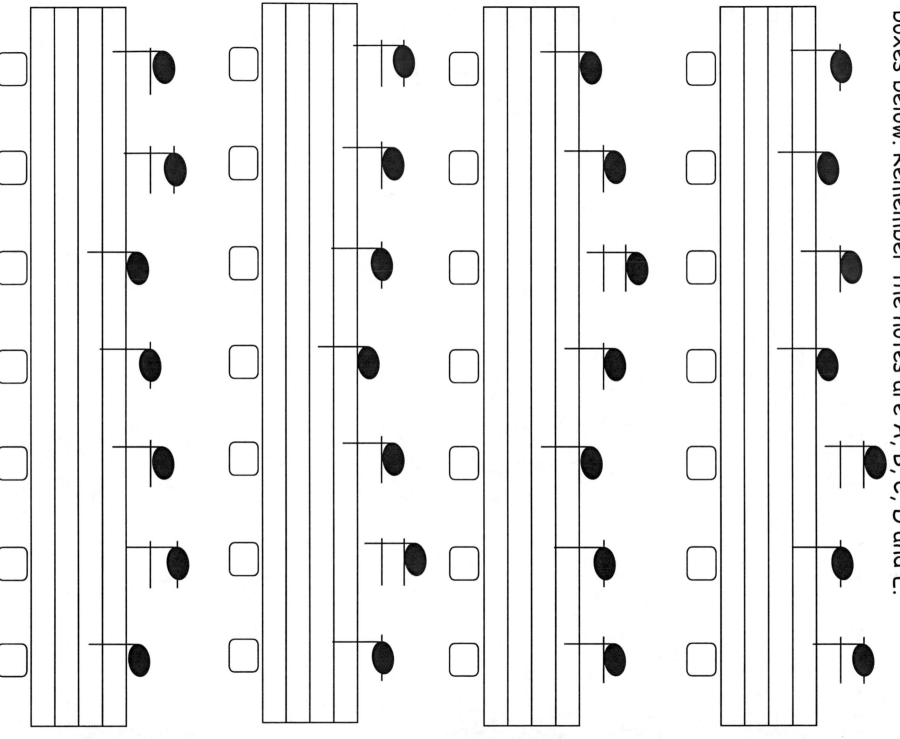

35

Draw the high notes (A, B, C, D, E) using the note names below. If the note is a High B, C, D or E, you will need to draw leger lines for the note to go on.

B   A   <u>B</u>   <u>D</u>   A   <u>B</u>   A

<u>C</u>   <u>A</u>   <u>D</u>   <u>A</u>   <u>E</u>   <u>B</u>   A

<u>D</u>   <u>B</u>   <u>E</u>   <u>B</u>   A   <u>D</u>   <u>B</u>

<u>E</u>   <u>A</u>   <u>B</u>   <u>D</u>   <u>B</u>   <u>A</u>   <u>B</u>

36

Draw the high notes using the note names below.
If the note is a High B, C, D, or E, you will need to
draw leger lines for the note to go on.

D B A B A E B

E A B D B A E

B E A B D A B

A B E B D B A

LEARNING LOW NOTES

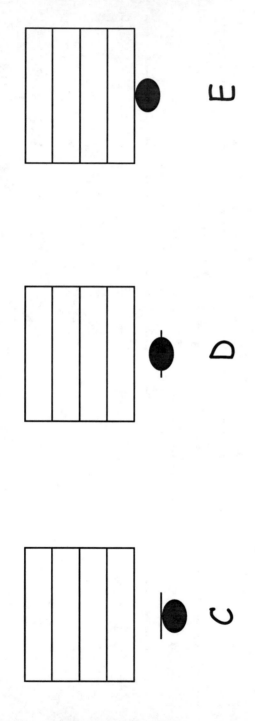

C   D   E

These notes are different because they are below the music staff.

Low C is on a space – 1 leger line below the staff

Low D is on a line – 1 leger line below the staff

Low E is on a space – below the staff

These are the low notes. Notice that the stems are facing up.

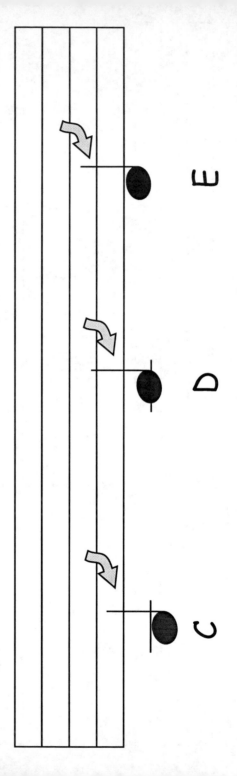

C   D   E

Draw the low 'C' note. Draw 1 leger line below the staff
and draw the note below that bottom leger line.

Draw the low 'D' note. Draw 1 leger line below the staff
and draw the note on that bottom leger line.

Draw the low 'E' note on the space below the staff.

Use these blank staves for practice.

Let's practice what you have learned. Write the note names below.

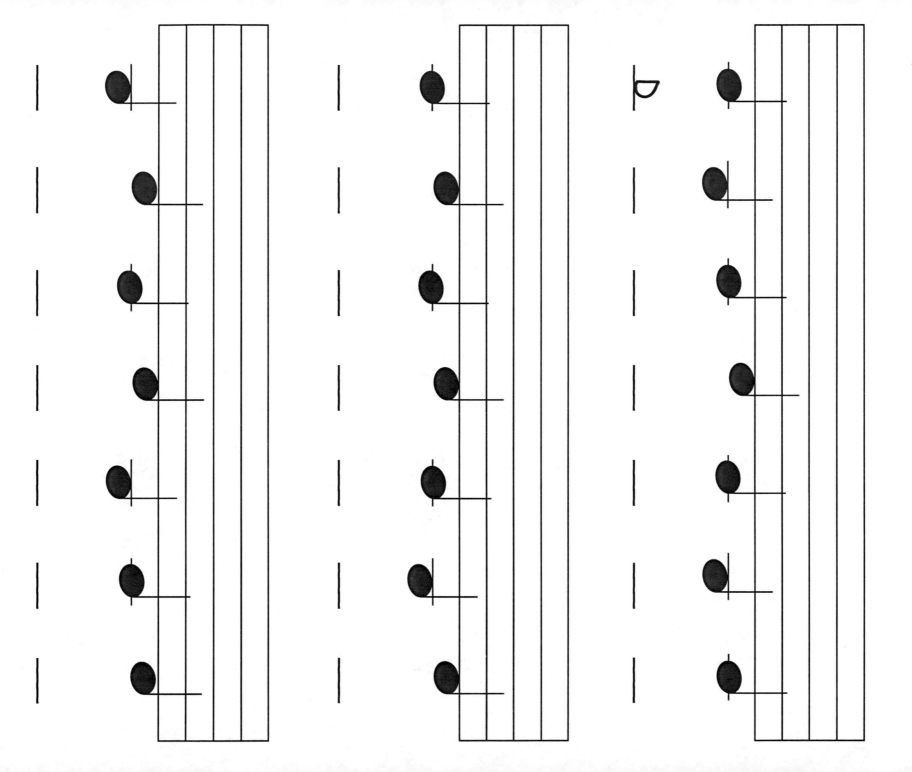

Write the note names below.

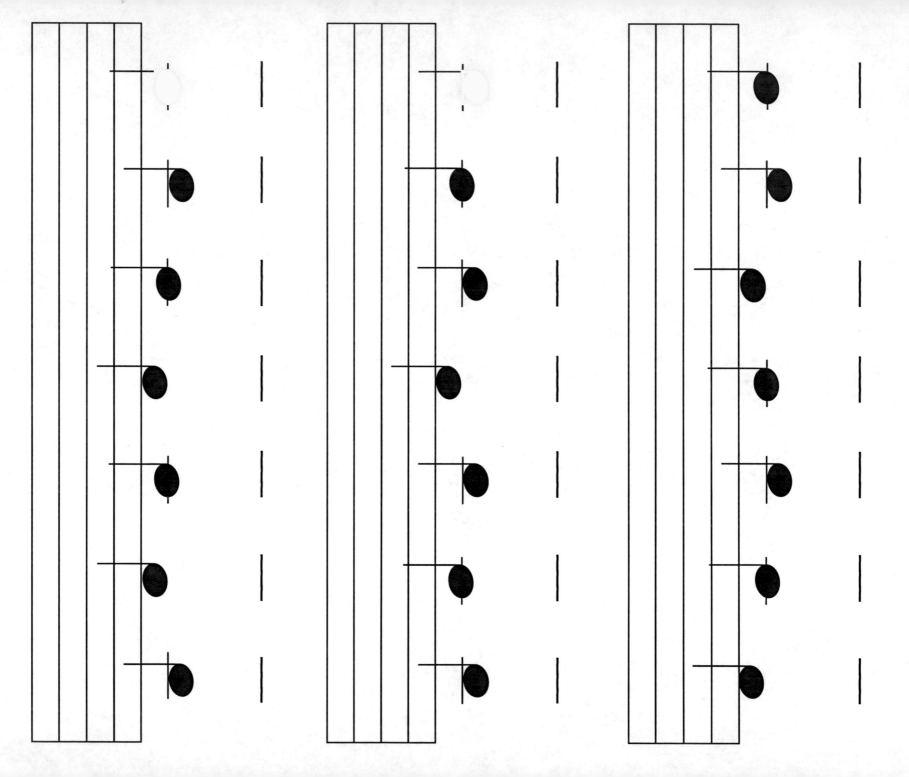

42

Draw the low note above each note name. If the note is a low C or D, you'll need to draw a leger line for the low note to go on.

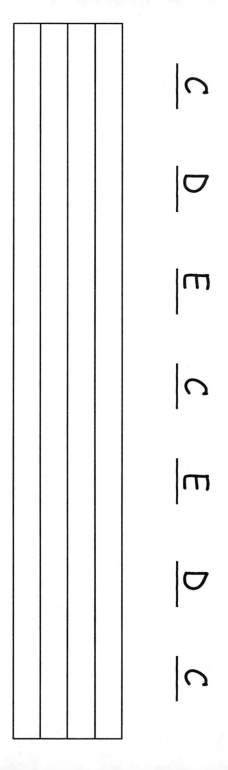

C D E C E D C

D E C E D C D

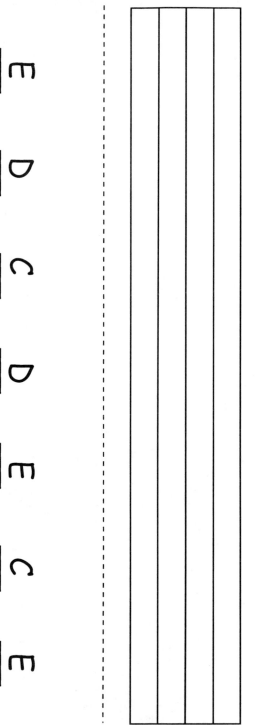

E D C D E C E

43

Draw the low note above each note name. If the note is a low C
or D, you'll need to draw a leger line for the low note to go on.

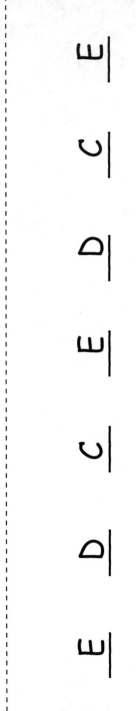

E   D   C   E   D   C   E

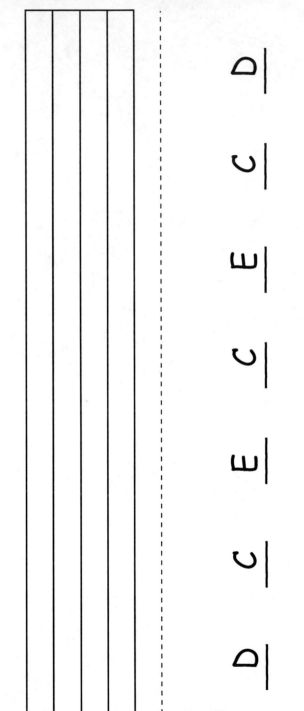

D   C   E   C   E   C   D

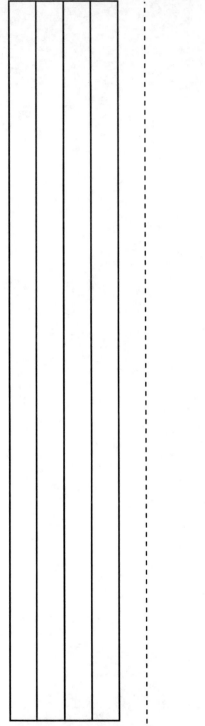

E   D   E   D   C   D   E

Here are all the notes we know.

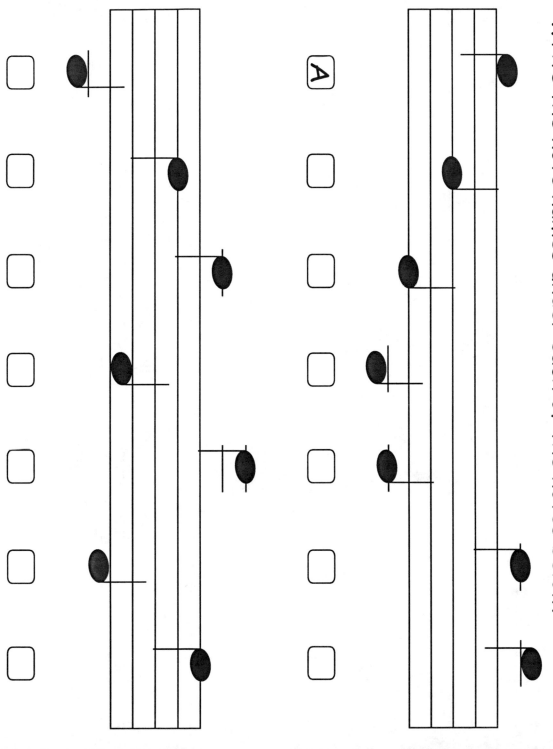

WOW – 17 Notes!

REVIEW OF ALL 17 NOTES

Write the note names under each of the notes below.

45

Write the note names under each of the notes below.

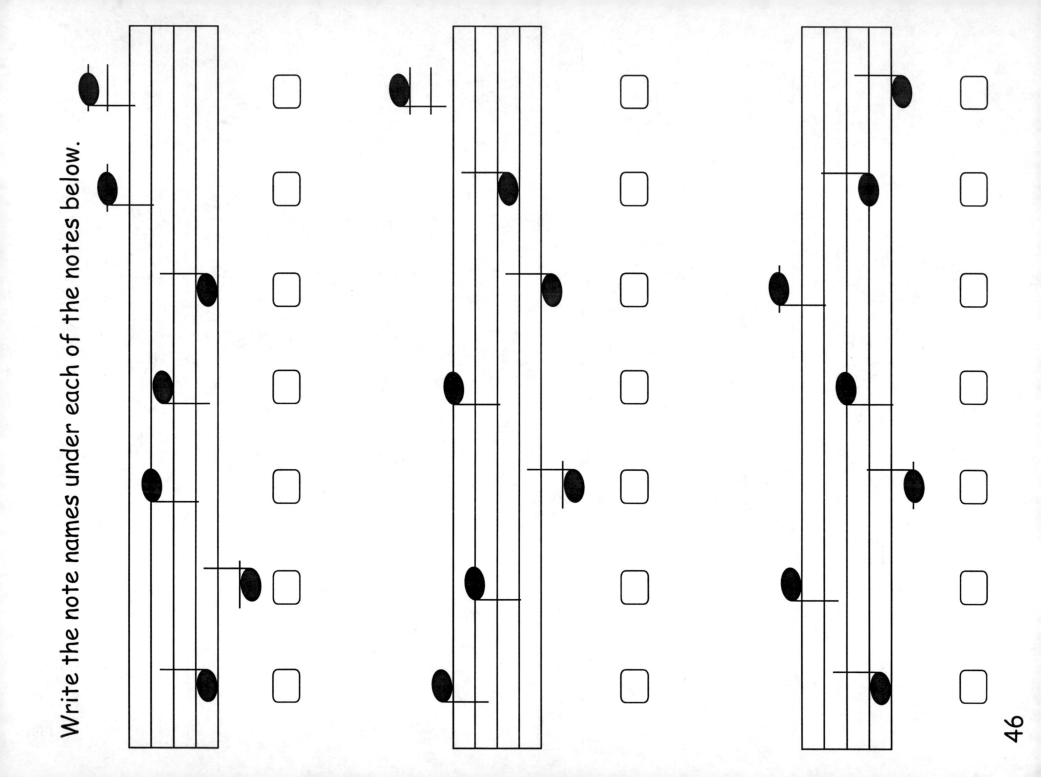

Write the note names under each of the notes below.

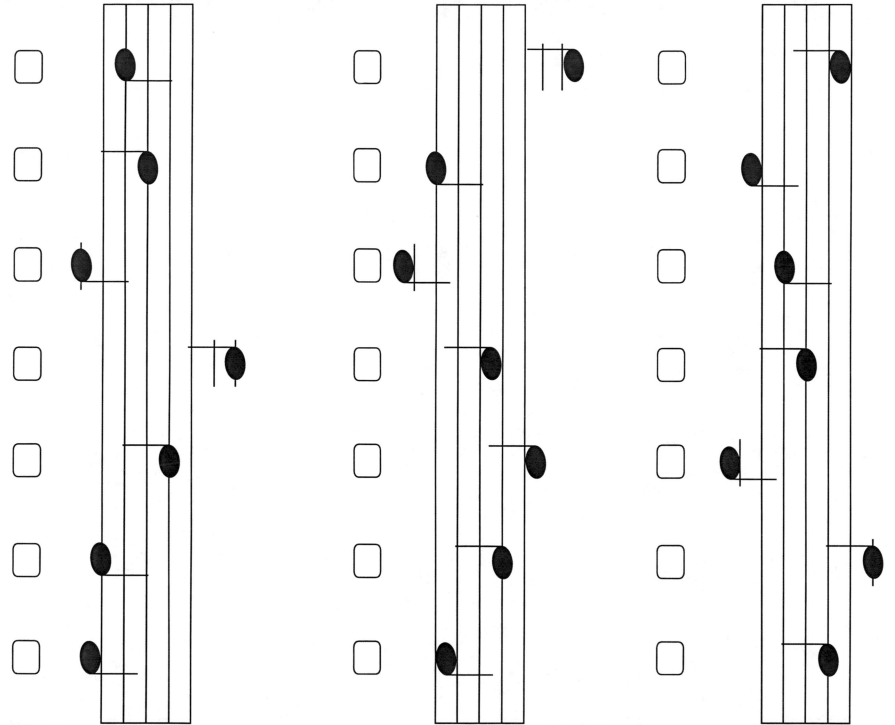

47

Write the note names under each of the notes below.

Write the note names under each of the notes below.

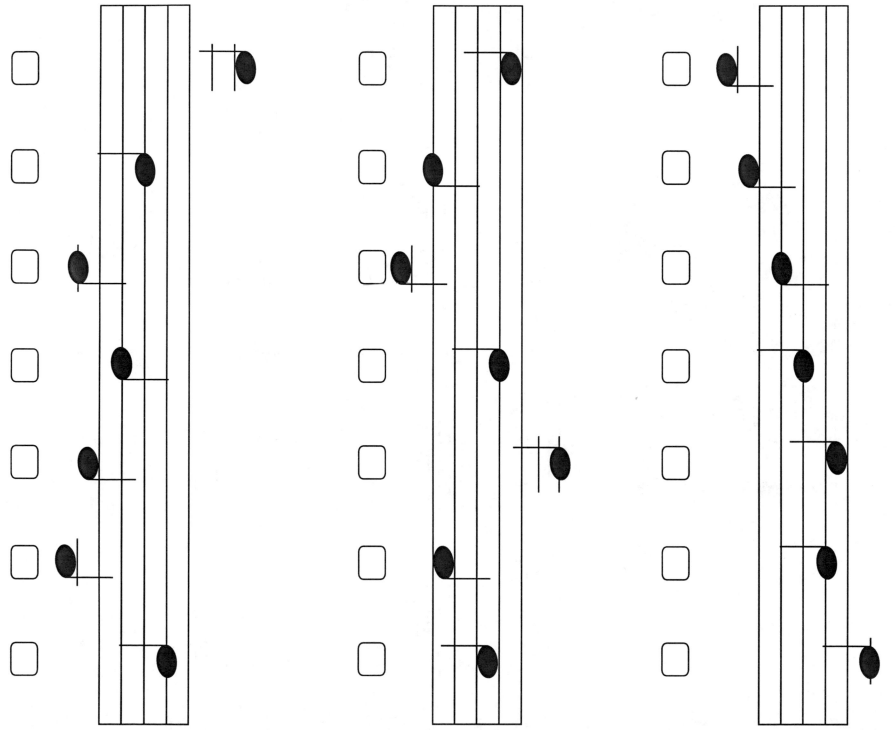

49

CROSSWORD PUZZLE

HOW OUR FINGERS PLAY NOTES
ON THE VIOLA

The Viola has 4 strings

C   G   D   A

String C
String G
String D
String A

Children **G**et **D**essert **A**lways

1   2   3   4

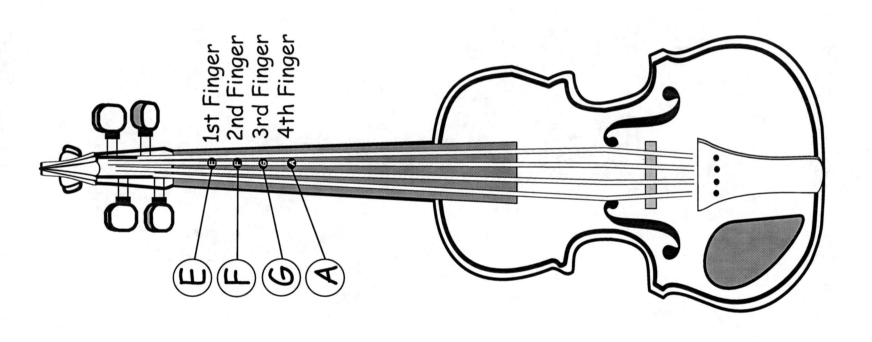

1st Finger
2nd Finger
3rd Finger
4th Finger

E F G A

NOTES ON THE 'D' STRING

Now that we know all the notes, we can learn where our fingers go when we read music.

Let's start with notes on the 'D' string.

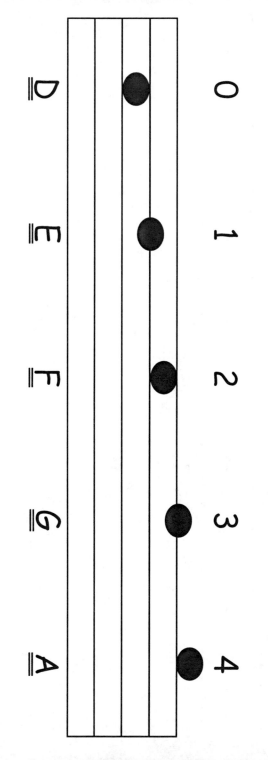

0   1   2   3   4

D   E   F   G   A

We play the 'D' with no fingers.
'D' is the open D string

We play the 'E' with our 1st finger (index).
We play the 'F' with our 2nd finger (middle).
We play the 'G' with our 3rd finger (ring).
We play the 'A' with our 4th finger (pinky).

Write the note names below the notes and the finger for those notes on the top.

54

Write the note names below the notes and the finger for those notes on the top.

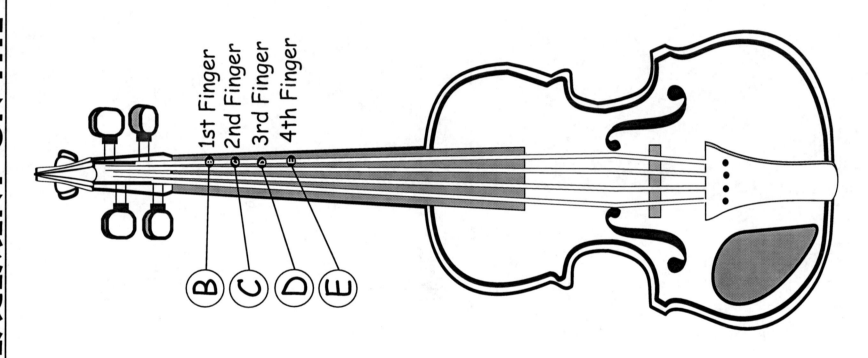

1st Finger
2nd Finger
3rd Finger
4th Finger

B   C   D   E

NOTES ON THE 'A' STRING

Let's continue with the 'A' string.

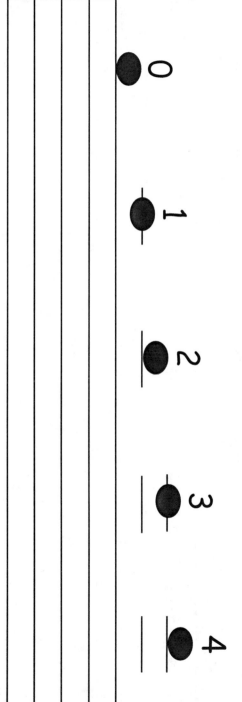

We play the 'A' with no fingers,
therefore 'A' is the open <u>A string</u>

We play the 'B' with our 1st finger (index).
We play the 'C' with our 2nd finger (middle).
We play the 'D' with our 3rd finger (ring).
We play the 'E' with our 4th finger (pinky).

Write the note names below the notes and the finger for those notes on the top.

Write the note names below the notes and the finger for those notes on the top.

Write the note names below the notes and the finger for those notes on the top.

Write the note names below the notes and the finger for those notes on the top.

D AND A STRING NOTES COMBINED

Write the note names underneath and the fingers you use on top.

D AND A STRING NOTES COMBINED

Write the note names underneath and the fingers you use on top.

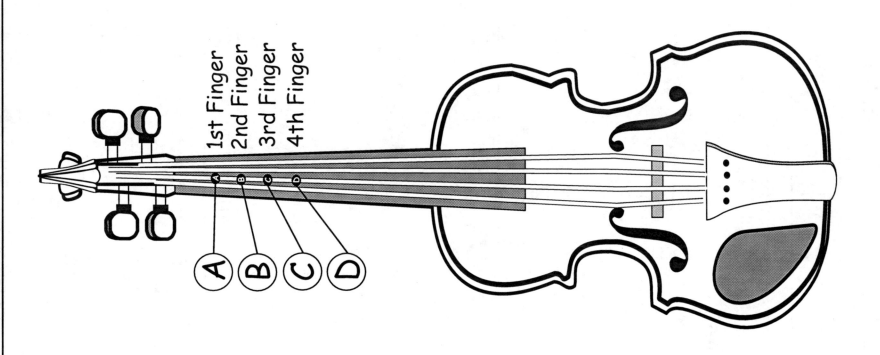

1st Finger
2nd Finger
3rd Finger
4th Finger

A B C D

NOTES ON THE 'G' STRING

Let's continue with the 'G' string.

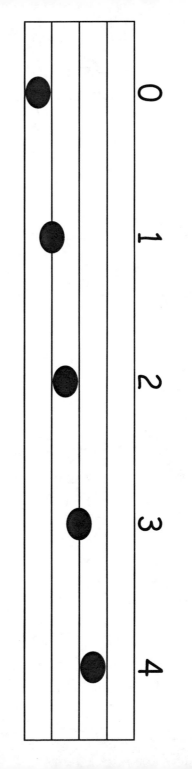

0   1   2   3   4

G   A   B   C   D

We play the 'G' with no fingers,
therefore 'G' is the open G string

We play the 'A' with our 1st finger (index).
We play the 'B' with our 2nd finger (middle).
We play the 'C' with our 3rd finger (ring).
We play the 'D' with our 4th finger (pinky).

Write the note names below the notes and the finger for those notes on the top.

O

G

68

Write the note names below the notes and the finger for those notes on the top.

Write the note names below the notes and the finger for those notes on the top.

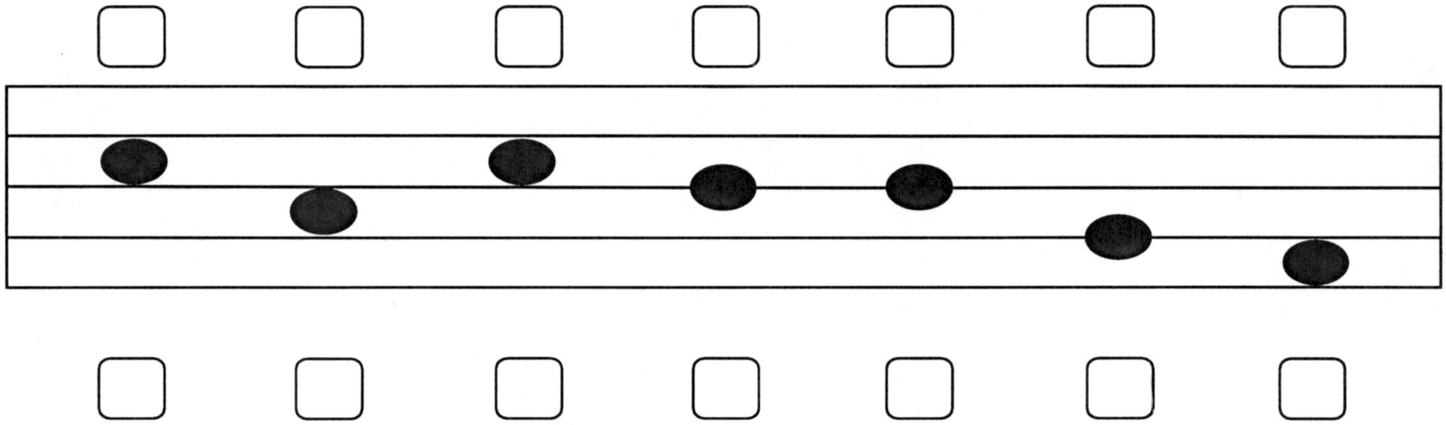

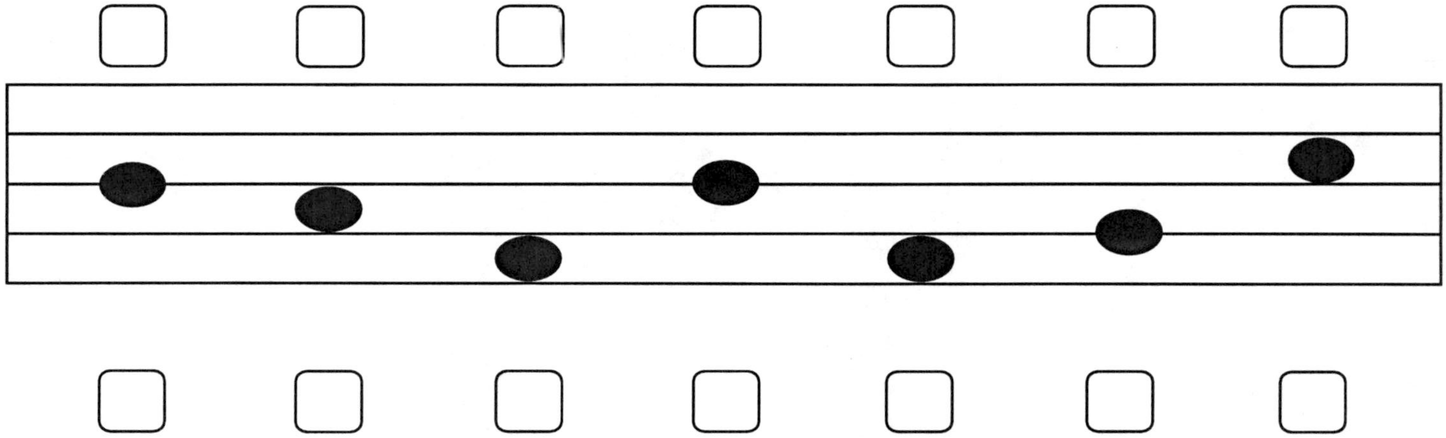

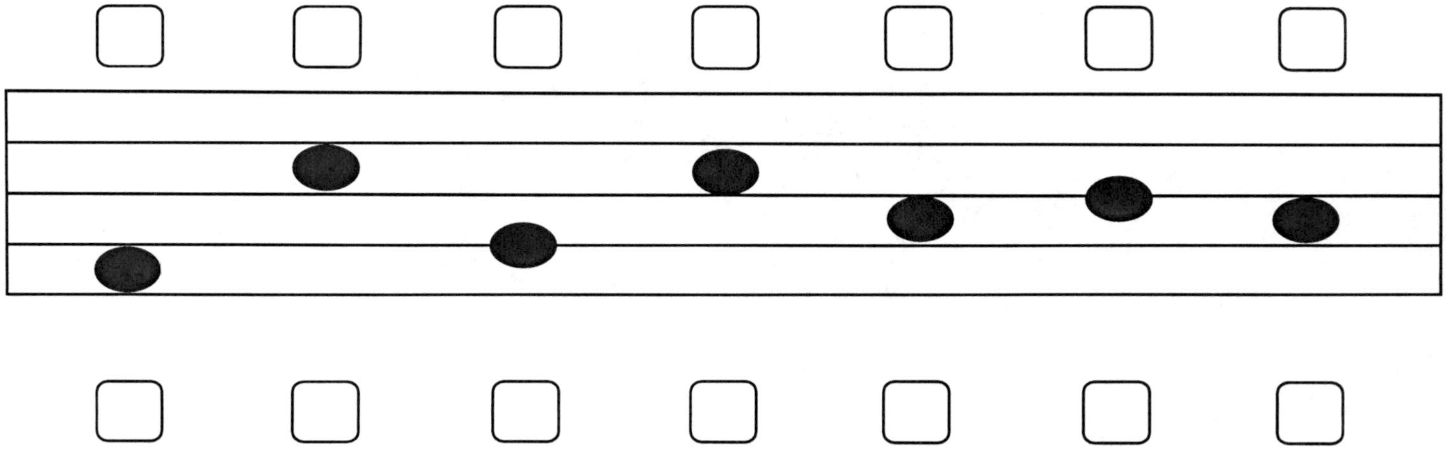

FINGER PLACEMENT ON THE 'C' STRING

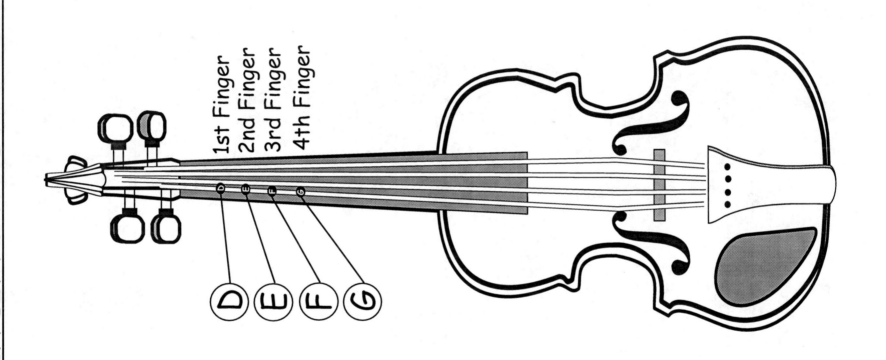

1st Finger
2nd Finger
3rd Finger
4th Finger

D E F G

NOTES ON THE 'C' STRING

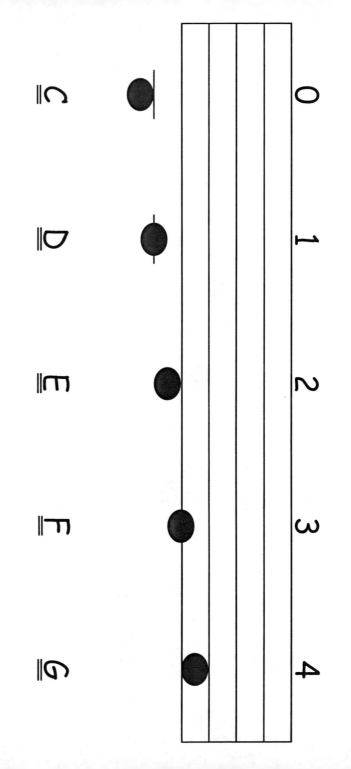

0   1   2   3   4

C   D   E   F   G

We play the 'C' with no fingers,
therefore 'C' is the open C string

We play the 'D' with our 1st finger (index).
We play the 'E' with our 2nd finger (middle).
We play the 'F' with our 3rd finger (ring).
We play the 'G' with our 4th finger (pinky).

73

Write the note names below the notes and the finger for those notes on the top.

Write the note names below the notes and the finger for those notes on the top.

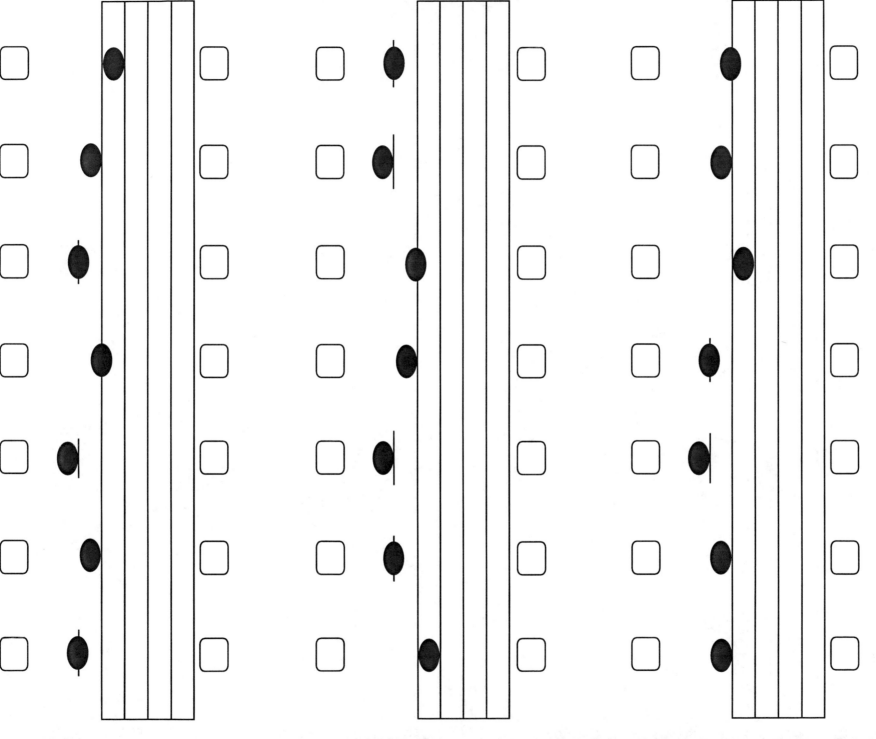

75

Write the note names below the notes and the finger for those
notes on the top.

Write the note names below the notes and the finger for those notes on the top.

G AND C STRING NOTES COMBINED

Write the note names below the notes and the finger for those notes on the top.

C AND G STRING NOTES COMBINED

Write the note names below the notes and the finger for those notes on the top.

USING ALL THE STRINGS

Write the note names on the bottom and the fingers you would use on the top. Be careful. These notes are on all of the strings!

Write the note names on the bottom and the fingers you use on the top.

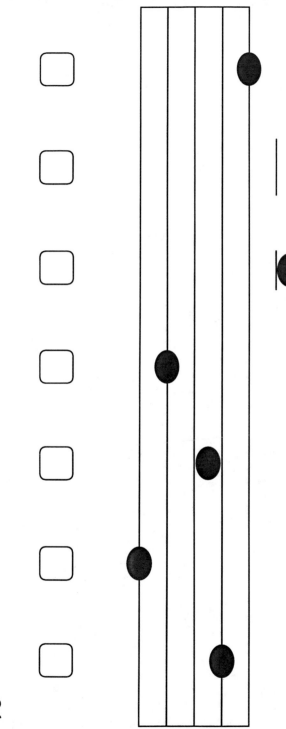
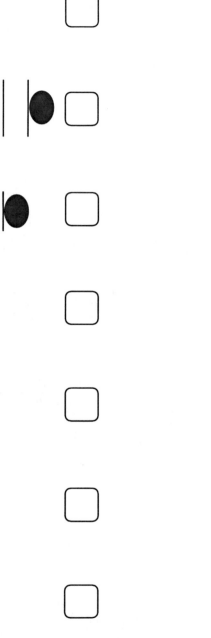
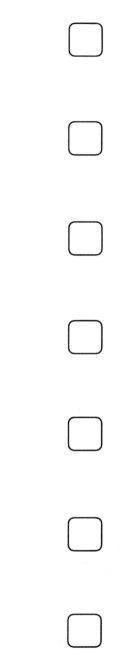
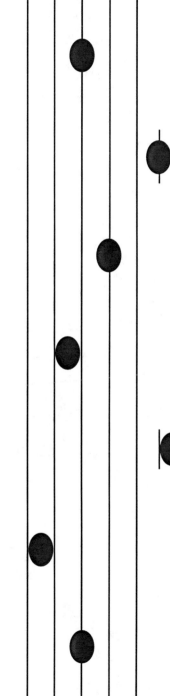

Write the note names on the bottom and the fingers you use on the top.

Write the note names on the bottom and the fingers you use on the top.

Write the note names on the bottom and the fingers you use on the top.

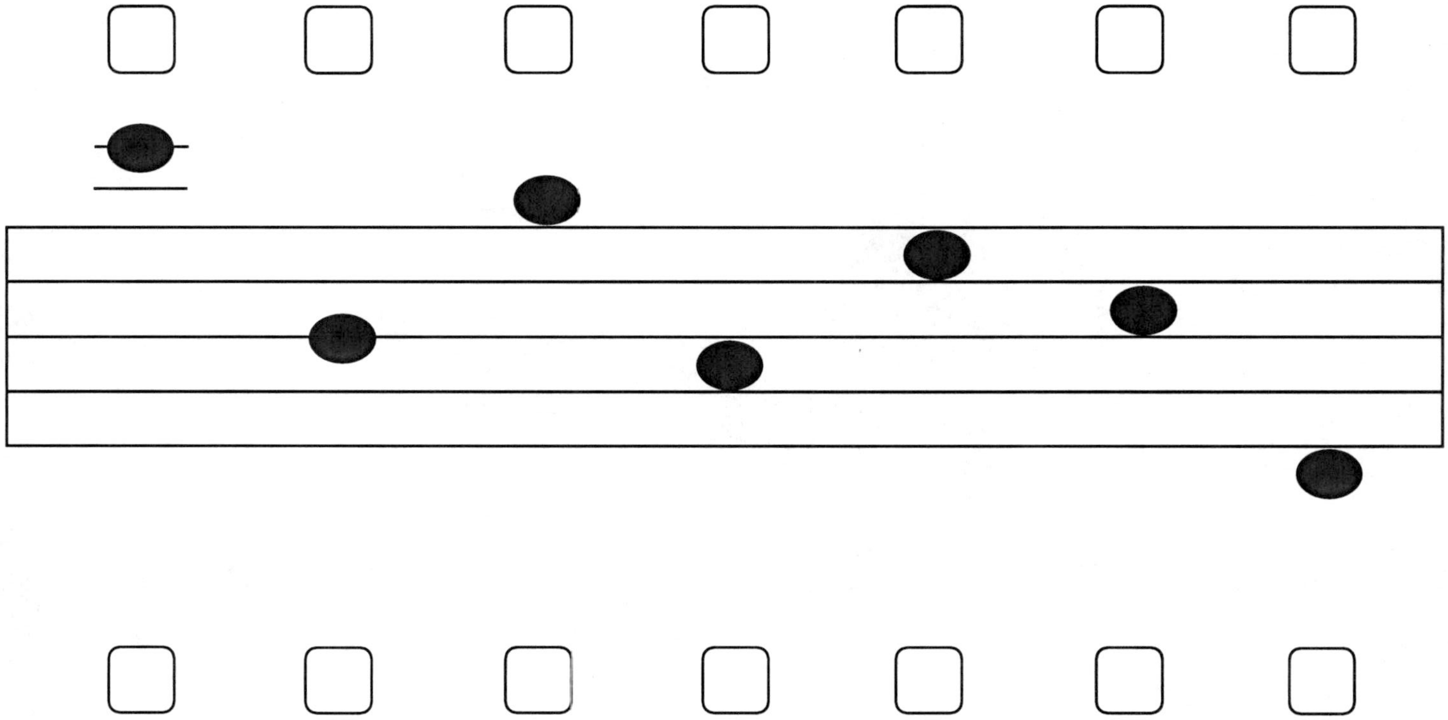

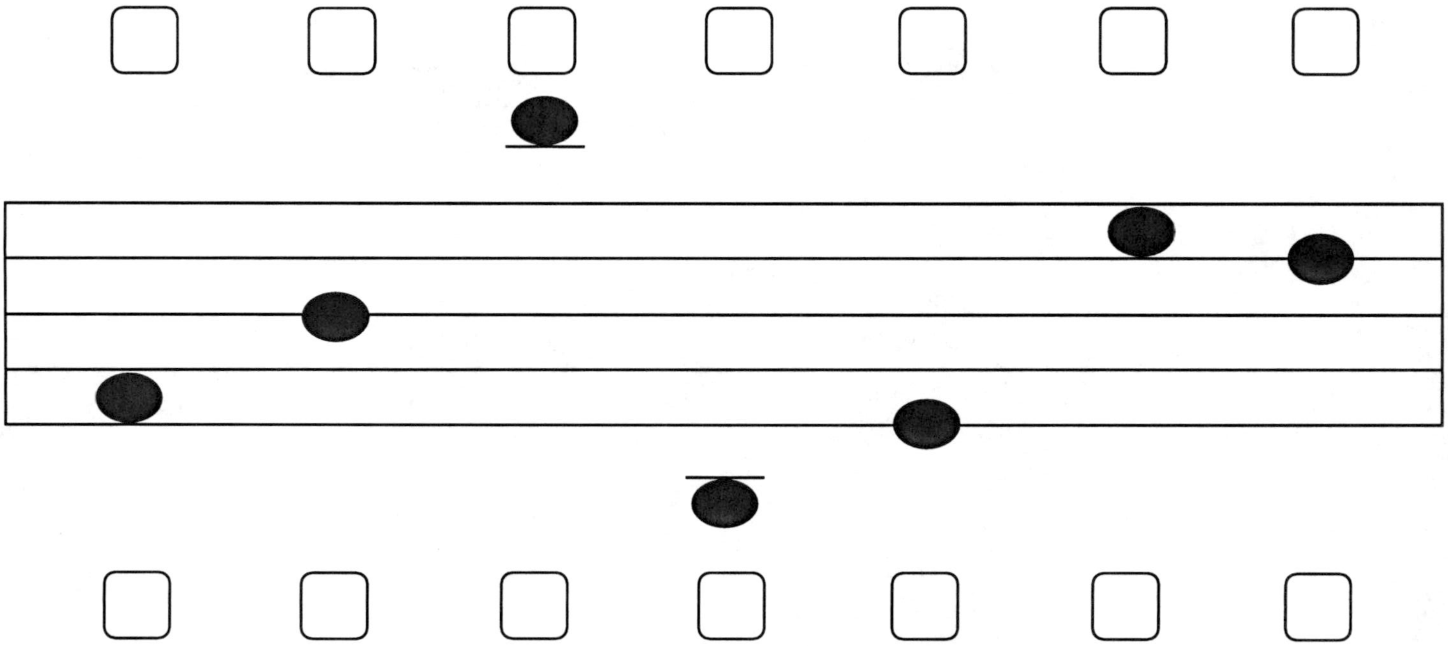

LEARNING NOTE TIMES

QUARTER NOTE

I have 1 beat

EIGHTH NOTE

I am quick.
I have a beat!

SIXTEENTH NOTE

I am really quick.
I have   beat!

WHOLE NOTE

I have 4 beats!

DOTTED HALF NOTE

I have 3 beats

HALF NOTE

I have 2 beats

LET'S REVIEW

A Whole Note gets ____ beats.

A Half Note gets ____ beats.

A Dotted Half Note gets ____ beats.

A Quarter Note gets ____ beats.

A Eighth Note gets ____ beats.

A Sixteenth Note gets ____ beats.

Draw a:

Whole Note ____

Half Note ____

Dotted Half Note ____

Quarter Note ____

Eighth Note ____

Sixteenth Note ____

How many beats does each note have?

♪ = ____ beats.

♩ = ____ beats.

𝅗𝅥 = ____ beats.

𝅝 = ____ beats.

𝅘𝅥𝅯 = ____ beats.

𝅗𝅥. = ____ beats.

In the box beside each note, write how many beats that note has.

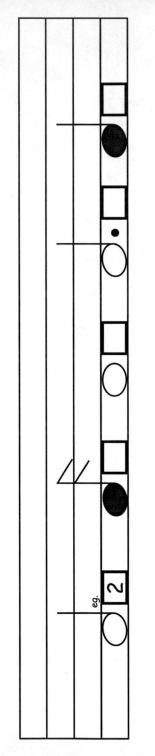
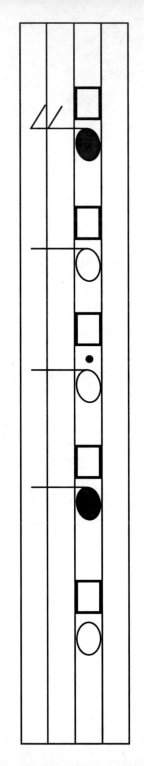
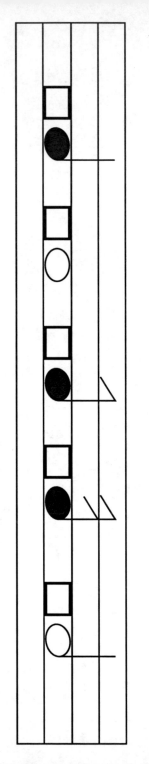
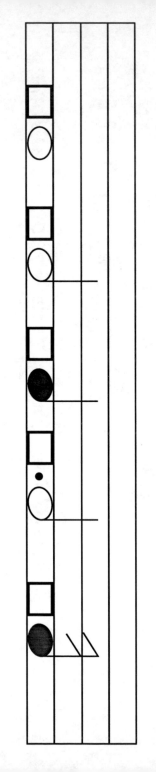

The notes we know so far are

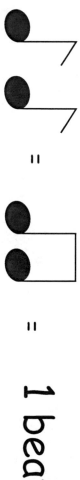

Before we start the next section there are 2 new combinations of notes we must learn:

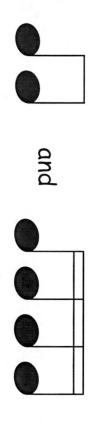 and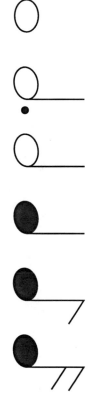

EIGHTH NOTES

When we put 2 eighth notes together, we join them with a line.

♪♪ = ♫ = 1 beat

These notes are fast and equal 1 beat.

SIXTEENTH NOTES

When we put 2 sixteenth notes together, we join them with 2 lines.

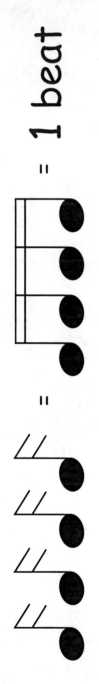

These notes are fast and equal beat.

When we put 4 sixteenth notes together, we join them with 2 lines.

= 1 beat

A NEW CONCEPT

4 sixteenth notes are the same as 2 eighth notes or 1 quarter note.

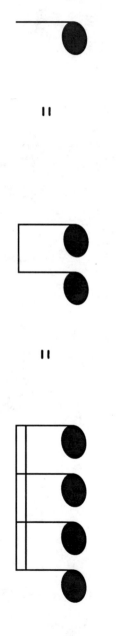

🕷 These all have 1 beat.

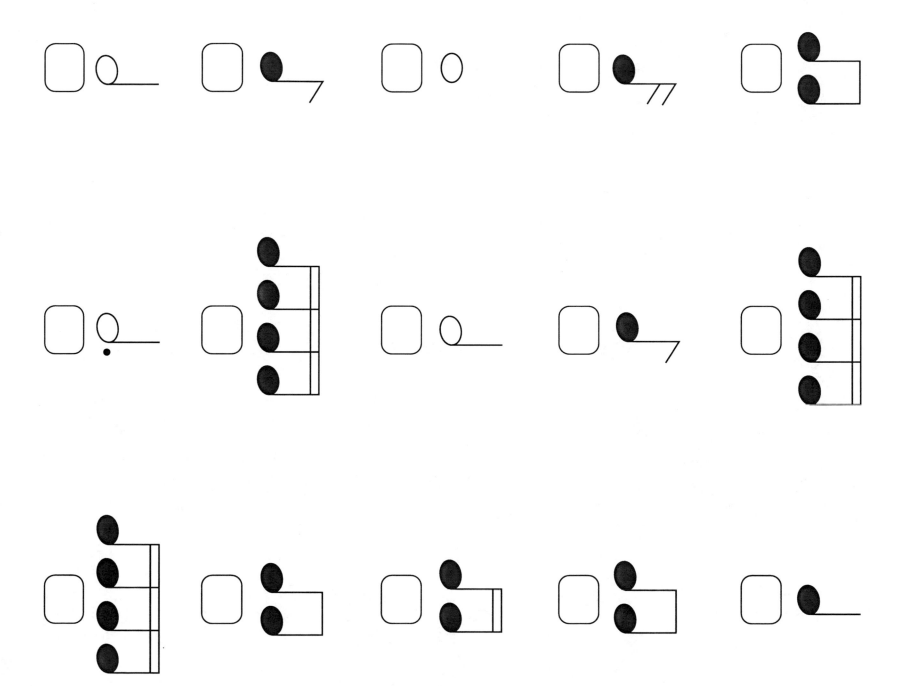

NOTE COMBINATION PRACTICE

Write under each example how may beats it has.

91

NOTE COMBINATION PRACTICE

Write under each example how may beats it has.

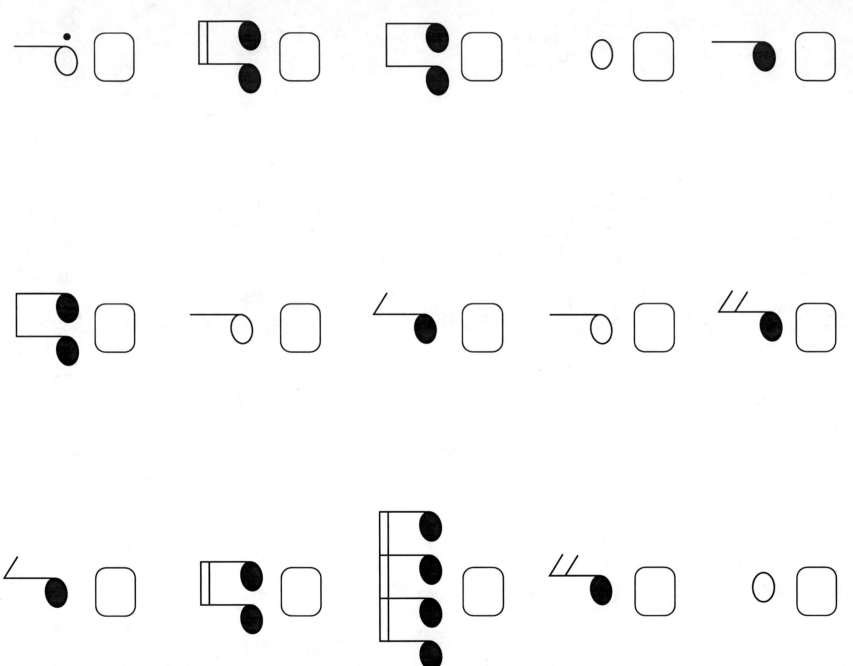

LEARNING REST VALUES

A rest is a pause where you are quiet just like a mouse.

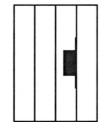

Whole Rest

I look like an upside down hat.

I have **4 beats** of quiet.

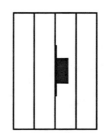

Half Rest

I look like a hat.

I have **2 beats** of quiet.

Quarter Rest

I have **1 beat** of quiet.

Eighth Rest

I have **½ a beat** of quiet.

Sixteenth Rest

I have a really quick quiet time.

I have **¼ of a beat.**

Here is an easy way to remember which is a half rest and which is a whole rest:

A half rest = ▬ = 2 beats. It looks like a hat.

A whole rest = ▬ = 4 beats. It looks like an upside down hat.

An upside down hat ▬ can fit more candy into it than a normal hat can.
▬

93

LET'S REVIEW

A Whole Rest gets ____ beats.

A Half Rest gets ____ beats.

A Quarter Rest gets ____ beats.

A Eighth Rest gets ____ beats.

A Sixteenth Rest gets ____ beats.

Draw a:

Whole Rest _____

Half Rest _____

Quarter Rest _____

Eighth Rest _____

Sixteenth Rest _____

How many beats
does each rest have?

▬ = ____ beats.

▬ = ____ beats.

𝄽 = ____ beats.

𝄾 = ____ beats.

𝄿 = ____ beats.

94

LET'S REVIEW

Match the following rest names with the correct drawing.

whole rest

half rest

quarter rest

eighth rest

sixteenth rest

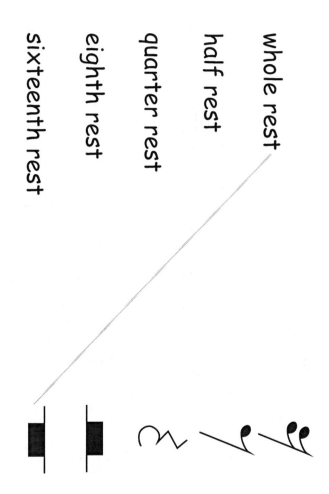

Match the following rest names with their correct beats of quiet.

whole rest   2

half rest   1/2

quarter rest   4

eighth rest   1

sixteenth rest   1/4

USING YOUR HAND

Now we'll put together everything we know

- Note Names
- Note Times
- Note Fingers

Write the note name below, the finger you use on the top, and write how many beats the note has in the box beside it.

<u>Example:</u>

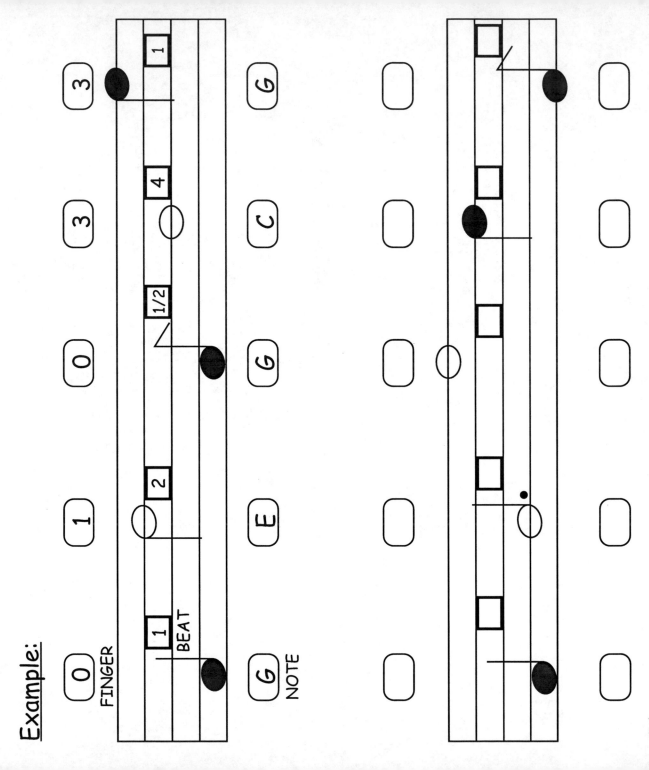

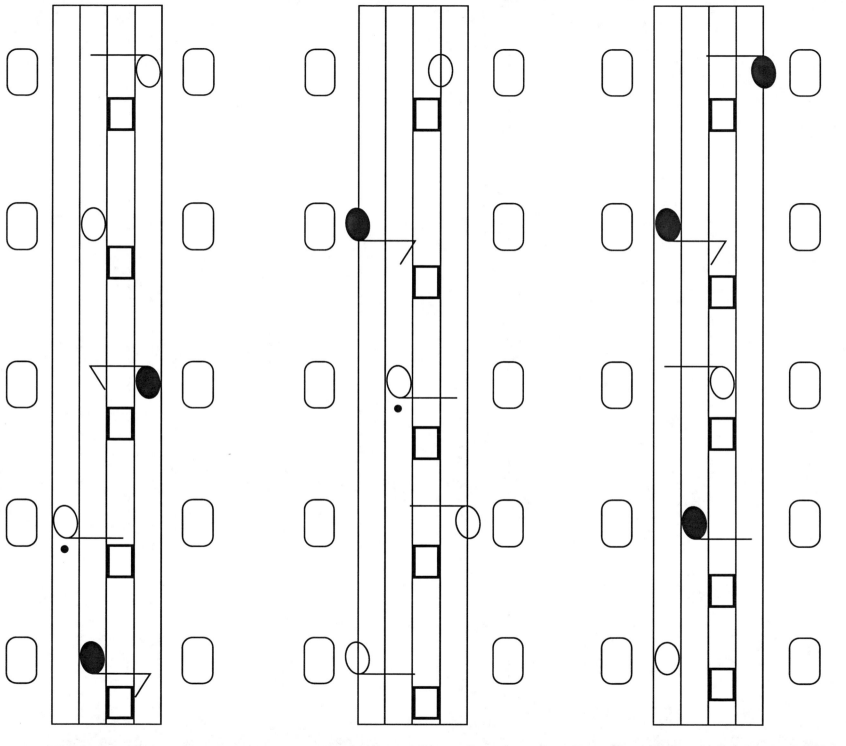

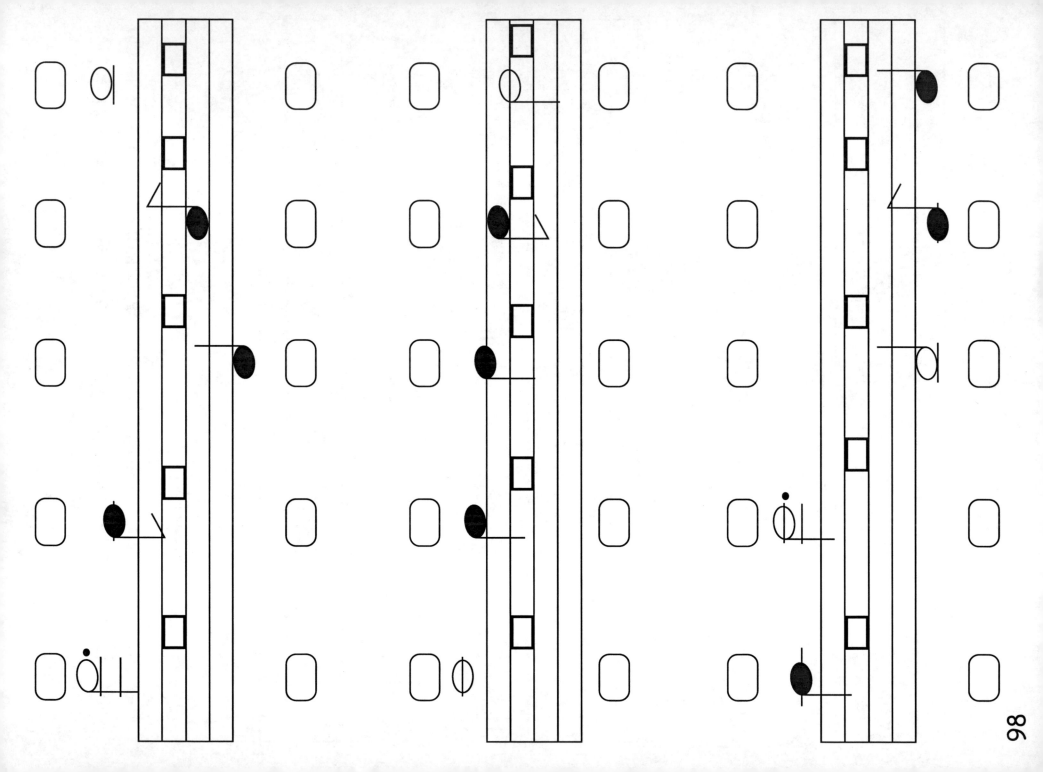

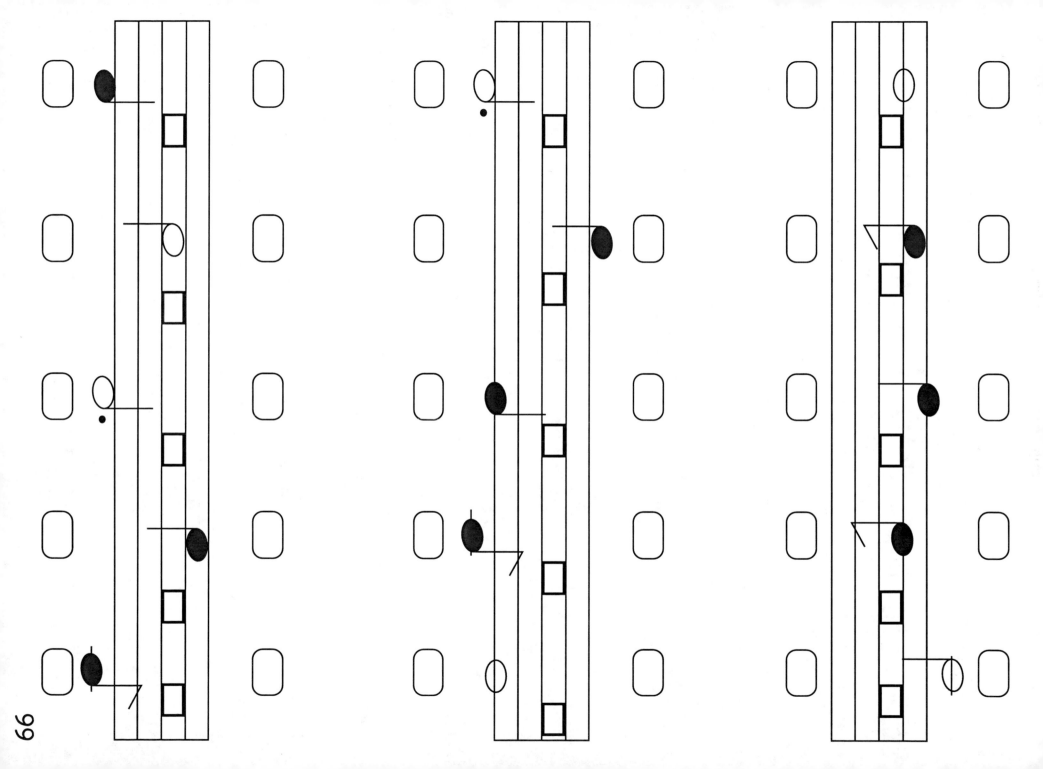

LEARNING ABOUT TIME SIGNATURES

In music, some notes sound strong and others sound weak. These strong and weak sounds are called beats. A bar line separates the beats. A double bar line at the end of the music tells us the song is over.

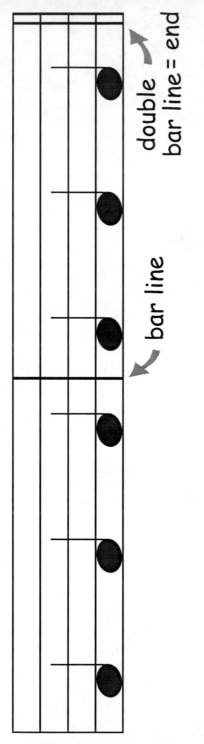

bar line

double
bar line = end

The notes and rests in between each set of bar lines are called a **measure** or **bar**.

Under each bar, write how many beats there are in total.

 Remember – each bar will have a different combination of notes but they should all have the same number of beats.

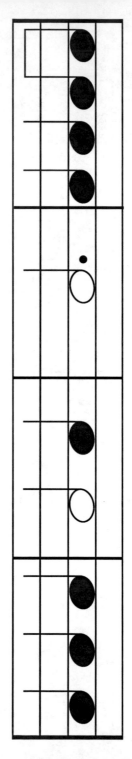

1+1+1 [ ]

2+1 [ ]

[ ]

[ ]

100

How many beats are in each bar? Write the total in the box underneath each bar.

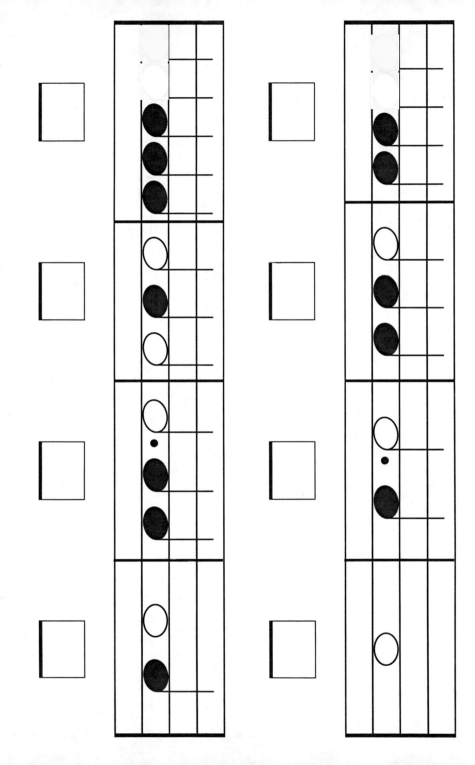

Let's make it tricky. Each bar can have both notes and rests. Count how many beats there are in each bar and write your answer in the box below.

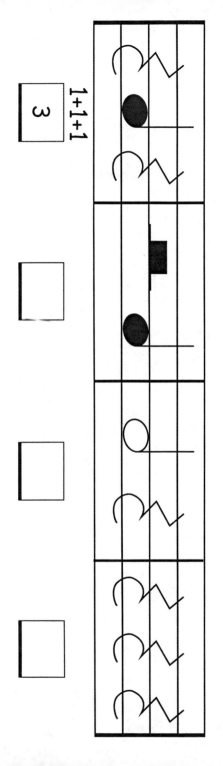

1+1+1

3

How many beats of both notes and rests are in each bar?
Write the number in the box underneath.

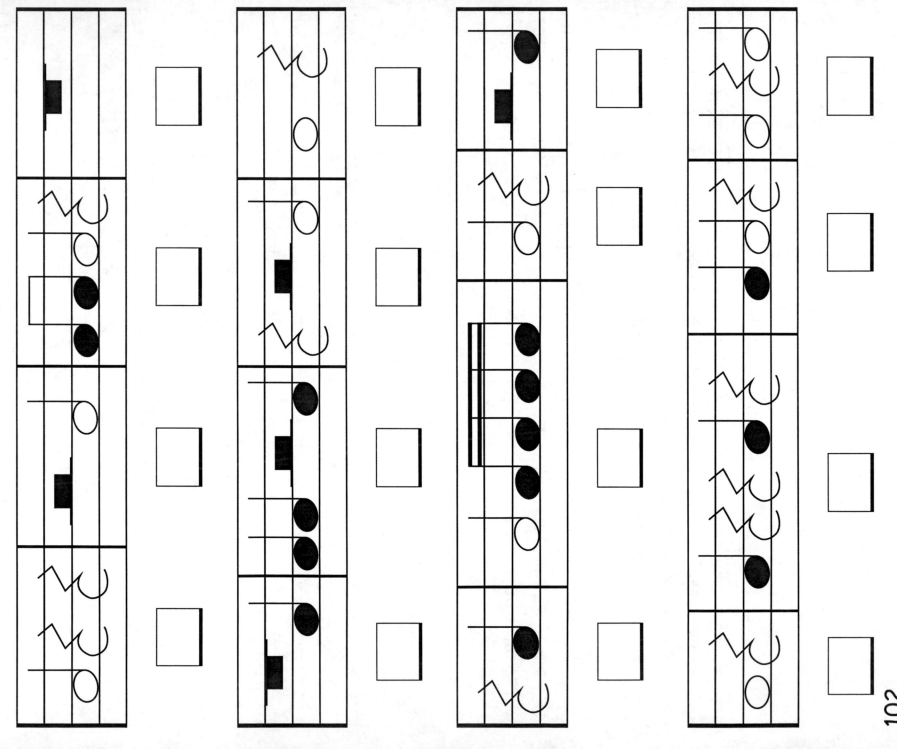

102

LEARNING TO WRITE TIME SIGNATURES

Time signatures are important because they tell us how many beats are in each bar.

To write time signatures, start at the beginning of the music. The time signature is always placed after any sharps or flats in the music.

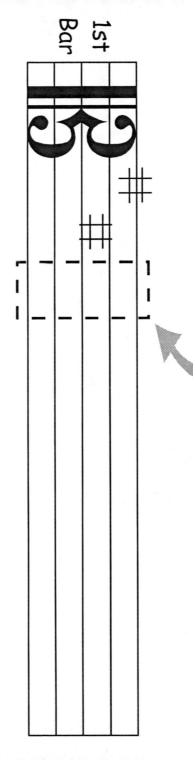

1st
Bar

The time signature of the song looks like this. It will have a number on top and a number on the bottom.

The top number tells you how many beats there are in each bar.

The bottom number tells you the kind of note that each bar combination will have.

Example #1

4 ← This means that there are 4 beats in each bar.

4 ← This means that the combination of beats must be equal to quarter notes (1 beat each).

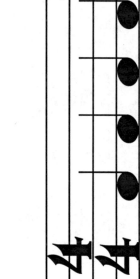

4 beats using 4 quarter notes

Note: $\frac{4}{4}$ time is called **quadruple time** or **common time** (*C*).

Example #2

3 ← This means that there are 3 beats in each bar.

4 ← This means the combinations of notes must be equal to the quarter notes.

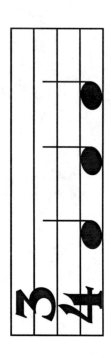

Note: $\frac{3}{4}$ time is called **triple time**.

104

Example #3

This means the combination of notes must be equal to quarter notes.

This means that there are 2 beats in each bar.

What is the time signature? Fill in the top blank space.
Count the beats in each bar and this will give you the top number.

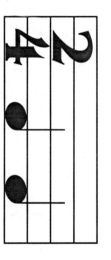

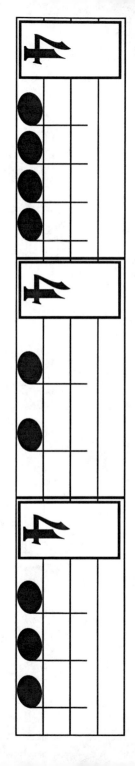

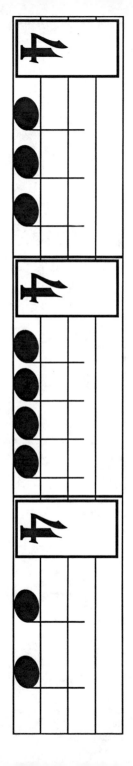

WRITING TIME SIGNATURES

Recall these examples:

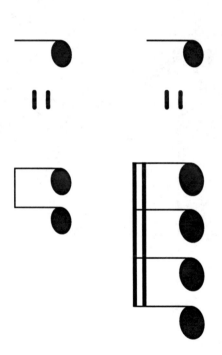

Using the above examples for help, fill in the top space with how many beats are in each bar. To help you, write the number of beats underneath each note then add them up.

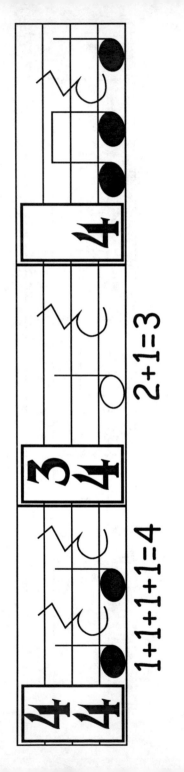
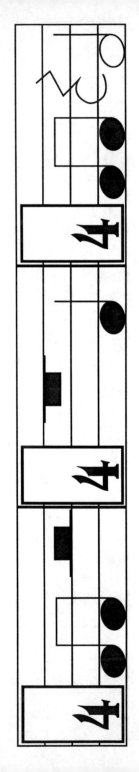

1+1+1+1=4

$$\frac{3}{4}$$

2+1=3

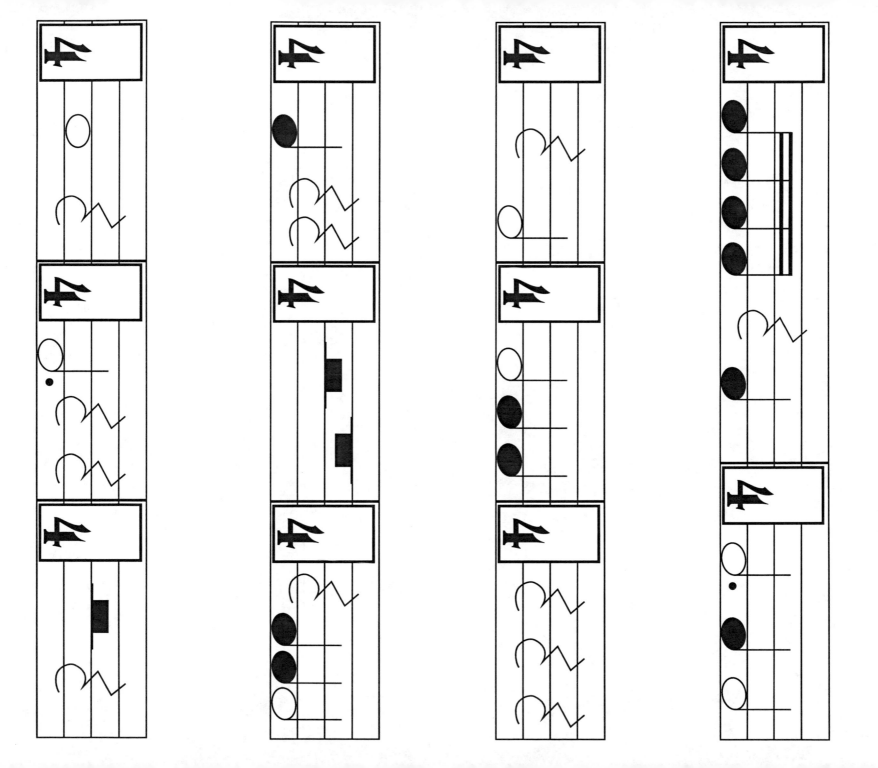

ADDING BAR LINES

Here is a new exercise. Add bar lines so each bar will have a certain number of beats.

Example

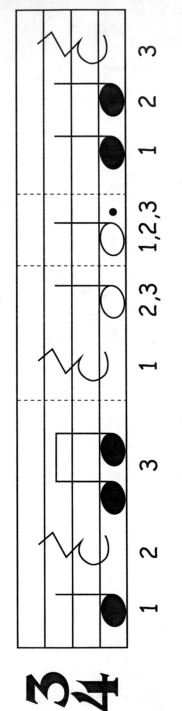

Notice how each bar line was drawn after 3 beats.

Try this on your own. If you do it correctly, each bar will equal 3 beats.

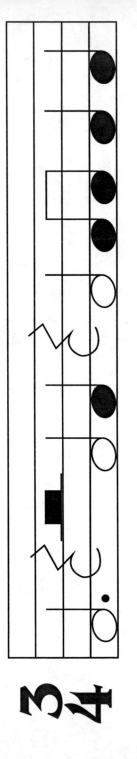

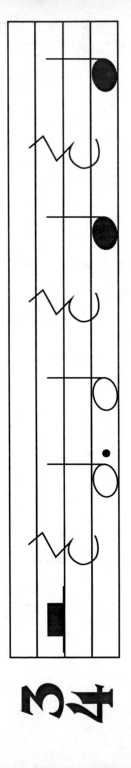

Now try adding bar lines with a new time signature. Each bar should have 4 beats.

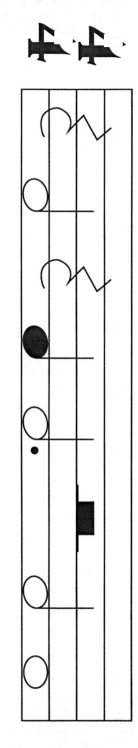

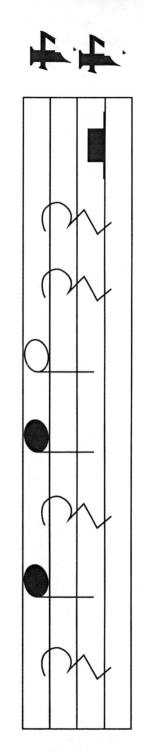

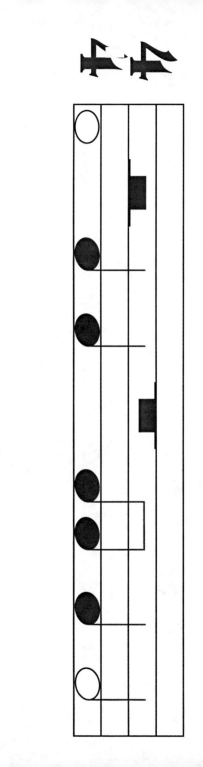

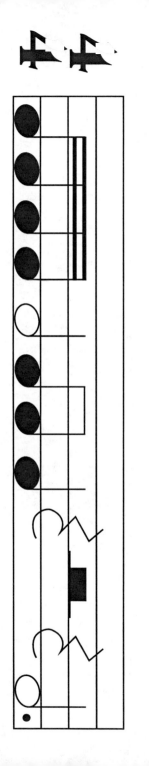

DRAWING YOUR OWN TIME SIGNATURES

Now it's your turn! Draw notes and rests in each bar.
You can choose any combination of notes and rests as long
as they equal the top number in the time signature.
Be sure to use different combinations of notes & rests.

Example

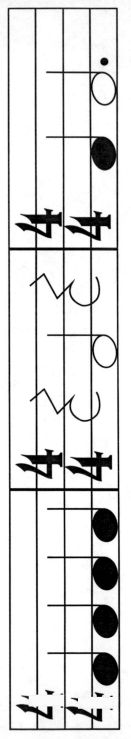

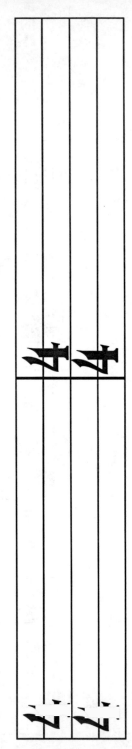

Make up your own combinations of notes and rests to fill each time signature.

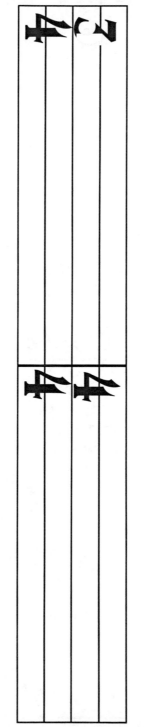

Make up your own combinations of notes and rests to fill each time signature.

$\begin{array}{c}2\\4\end{array}$

$\begin{array}{c}2\\4\end{array}$

$\begin{array}{c}2\\4\end{array}$

$\begin{array}{c}4\\4\end{array}$

$\begin{array}{c}4\\4\end{array}$

$\begin{array}{c}2\\4\end{array}$

$\begin{array}{c}3\\4\end{array}$

$\begin{array}{c}3\\4\end{array}$

$\begin{array}{c}2\\4\end{array}$

$\begin{array}{c}3\\4\end{array}$

$\begin{array}{c}3\\4\end{array}$

$\begin{array}{c}3\\4\end{array}$

Use this page for extra practice. Make up your own
time signatures.

LEARNING MUSICAL TERMS

To play cello, there are some musical terms and signs that you must know. Here are a few of them.

	crescendo	gradually louder
	decrescendo	gradually softer
	fermata	hold the note or rest longer
	tie	connects 2 notes of the same pitch
	slur	connects 2 notes of a different pitch
	flat	lowers the note a semitone or a half step
	sharp	raises the note a semitone or a half step
	natural sign	cancels out a sharp and flat
	bar line	vertical line separating the staff into measures
	repeat sign	go back to the beginning and play again
	piano	play softly
	forte	play loudly

Symbol	Term	Definition
𝅘𝅥.	staccato	short and detached note
mp	mezzopiano	medium or moderately soft
mf	mezzoforte	medium or moderately loud
𝄡	alto clef	at the beginning of each line of music
⊓	down bow	move your bow from the frog to the tip in a downward motion
⋁	up bow	move your bow from the tip to the frog in a upward motion
ff	fortissimo	very loud
pp	pianissimo	very soft
rit.	ritardando	gradually slow down
	music staff	the lines and spaces where the music notes are written

Match the musical term with the correct symbol.

decrescendo

bar line

fermata

repeat sign

slur

piano

sharp

tie

crescendo

forte

flat

natural sign

Match the musical term with the correct symbol.

⊞ (music staff grid)	alto clef
pp	down bow
V	staccato
B (alto clef)	music staff
mp	up bow
♪	pianissimo
mf	fortissimo
⊓	ritardano
ff	mezzopiano
rit.	mezzoforte

Beside the description, write the name of the musical term that is being described.

Natural Sign	cancels out a sharp and flat
	gradually louder
	vertical line separating the staff into measures
	hold the note or rest longer
	connecting 2 or more notes of different pitches
	play loudly
	connecting 2 notes of the same pitch
	lowers the note a semitone or half step
	gradually softer
	go back to the beginning and play again
	play softly
	raises the note a semitone or half step

Beside the description, write the name of the musical term that is being described.

_____ short and detached note

_____ medium or moderately soft

_____ medium or moderately loud

_____ at the beginning of each line of music

_____ move your bow from the frog to the tip in a downward motion

_____ move your bow from the tip to the frog in an upward motion

_____ very loud

_____ very soft

_____ gradually slow down

_____ the lines and spaces where the music notes are written

119

BOOK REVIEW

How many music spaces are there on the music staff? _____

How many lines are there on the music staff? _____

What is the 4 word saying to remember our space notes?

_____

What is the 5 word saying to remember our line notes?

_____

<u>Follow the instructions for each box:</u>

Draw a note with a stem that is down

Draw a note with a stem that is up

Draw a sharp.

Draw a flat.

Draw a natural sign

Draw a alto clef.

120

Circle the alto clef that is in the right place on the music staff.

Follow the instructions for each box:

Draw a quarter note

Draw an eighth note

Draw a half note

Draw a whole note

Draw a dotted half note

Draw a sixteenth note

How many beats does a ♩ note have? _____

How many beats does a ♩ note have? _____

How many beats does a ♩ note have? _____

How many beats does a ♪ note have? _____

How many beats does a ○ note have? _____

How many beats does a ♩. note have? _____

What is the name of this rest? ▬ _____

What is the name of this rest? ▬ _____

What is the name of this rest? 𝄽 _____

What is the name of this rest? 𝄾 _____

What is the name of this rest? 𝄿 _____

122

How many beats does a half rest have? _____

How many beats does a quarter note have? _____

How many beats does a whole rest have? _____

How many beats does a eighth note have? _____

How many beats does a sixteenth rest have? _____

Write the names of these notes on the line underneath.

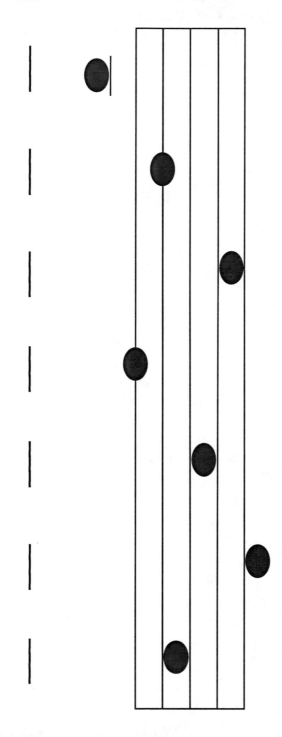

Write which fingers you would use for each note on the top
and the name of the note underneath.

Draw the 5 notes that can be played on the A string.
Write the name of the note underneath with the finger
you use on top.

Draw the 5 notes that can be played on the D string.
Write the name of the note underneath with the finger
you use on top.

125

Draw the 5 notes that can be played on the G string.
Write the name of the note underneath with the finger you use on top.

Draw the 5 notes that can be played on the C string.
Write the name of the note underneath with the finger you use on top.

Write the note name below, the finger you use on the top, and write how many beats the note has in the box beside it.

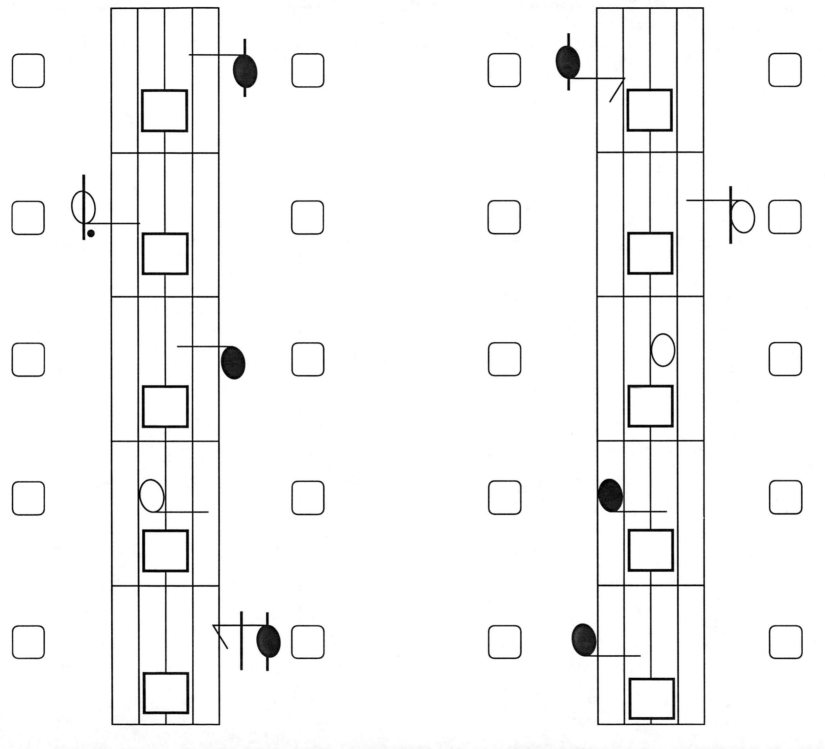

127

What is the time signature?

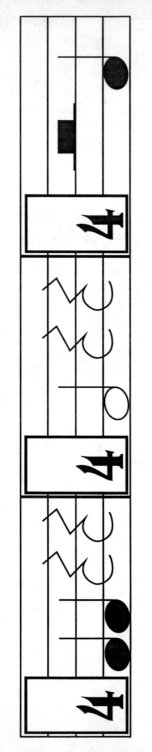

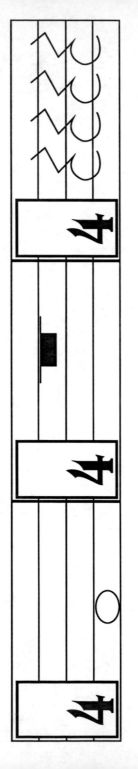

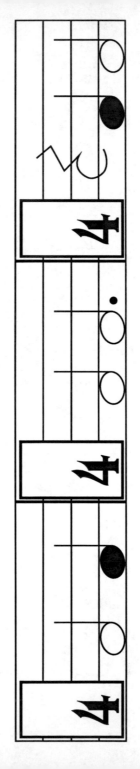

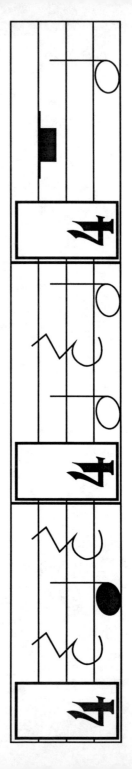

Fill in the time signatures using a combination of notes and rests that equal the time signature you see.

$\dfrac{3}{4}$ $\dfrac{4}{4}$ | $\dfrac{3}{4}$ $\dfrac{4}{4}$

$\dfrac{4}{4}$ $\dfrac{4}{4}$ | $\dfrac{4}{4}$ $\dfrac{4}{4}$

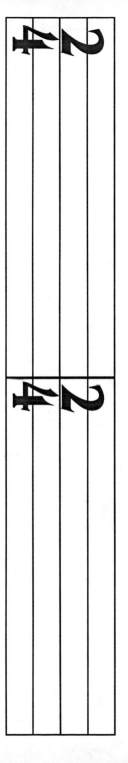

$\dfrac{2}{4}$ $\dfrac{4}{4}$ | $\dfrac{2}{4}$ $\dfrac{4}{4}$

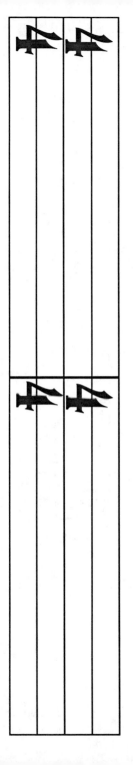

$\dfrac{4}{4}$ $\dfrac{4}{4}$ | $\dfrac{5}{4}$ $\dfrac{4}{4}$

MUSIC WORD SEARCH

```
H O R S E H A I R T U N E R S
N A C R E S C E N D O K A S V
A H B O W L E E T H A C I
T F R O G U H O M C H G L R O
U I S H A R P S U R E E F O L
R S P A C E A F S E O I R L A
A H U L I N E L I S R G E L N
L F E R M A T A C C Y H S O A
S O H H O T A T H E N T T W H
I R U P B O W H O N G H E H T
G T P A R I T A R D A N D O A
N E A S T R I N G O V O N L L
U Q U A R T E R R E S T O E T
H A L F N O T E H H C E T R O
A S T A C C A T O T I P E E C
W H O L E N O T E B I N S S L
A L M E Z Z O P I A N O R T E
B E V Q U A R T E R N O T E F
T D O W N B O W H L S T A F F
H A L U E F O R T I S S I M O
R E P E A T S I G N A M T U T
M E Z Z O F O R T E H A H R H
```

HORSEHAIR
STRING
TUNERS
BOW
QUARTER REST
DECRESCENDO
SLUR
EIGTH NOTE
FORTE
PIANO
MEZZOPIANO
DOWN BOW
QUARTER NOTE
STAFF
VIOLA
REPEAT SIGN
RITARDANDO
FORTISSIMO
UP BOW
TIE

ALTO CLEF
WHOLE REST
MEZZOFORTE
NOTES
HALF REST
SHARP
CRESCENDO
FERMATA
NATURAL SIGN
HALF NOTE
STACCATO
WHOLE NOTE
BAR LINE
MUSIC
SPACE
FLAT
LINE
THEORY
FROG
TIP
SCROLL

MELANIE SMITH

Melanie Smith has studied music since the age of three. Her training has been predominately on the violin and piano, however, she also plays the viola, cello and guitar. Throughout her violin career, Melanie studied classical, fiddle and jazz violin, as well as performed with the Edmonton Youth Orchestra, as a member of a quartet, and as a soloist.

The idea for this book arose from Melanie's experience as a violin teacher for young children. She found she needed a theory book that was specifically designed to complement violin instruction, while still allowing theory to be engaging and fun for her students.

CROSSWORD PUZZLE. ANSWER KEY

Across

1)
2)
3)
4)
5)
6)
7)
8)
9)
10)
11)

Down

12)
13)
14)
15)
16)
17)
18)
19)
20)
21)
22)

132

MUSIC WORD SEARCH
ANSWER KEY

Word list (left):

- ALTO CLEF
- WHOLE REST
- MEZZOFORTE
- NOTES
- HALF REST
- SHARP
- CRESCENDO
- FERMATA
- NATURAL SIGN
- HALF NOTE
- STACCATO
- WHOLE NOTE
- BAR LINE
- MUSIC
- SPACE
- FLAT
- LINE
- THEORY
- FROG
- TIP
- SCROLL

Word list (right):

- HORSEHAIR
- STRING
- TUNERS
- BOW
- QUARTER REST
- DECRESCENDO
- SLUR
- EIGTH NOTE
- FORTE
- PIANO
- MEZZOPIANO
- DOWN BOW
- QUARTER NOTE
- STAFF
- VIOLA
- REPEAT SIGN
- RITARDANDO
- FORTISSIMO
- UP BOW
- TIE

Certificate
of Accomplishment

This certifies that

_____

has successfully completed Book Two

Beginner Viola Theory

for Children workbook

_____ Teacher

_____ Date